Scribes Trained
for the Kingdom

A Pre-Grammar for
New Testament Greek
as a
Spiritual Discipline

A 10-Week Short-Course
for English Bible Readers

by
Gary D. Collier

1st Edition

△The *Dialogē* Press
ἡ διαλογή
452 W Water St
Cloverdale, IN. 46120
August 2019

Translations: Unless indicated otherwise, translations of ancient Greek and Hebrew texts are by the author based on the standard texts listed in the Abbreviations section.

Book and Cover design: The Dialogē Press. The cover art is a mosaic above the entrance to the cave of the traditional site where John, in exile on the Island of Patmos, received his revelation and dictated it to his scribe Prochoros. Picture by Richard E. Davies.

Citation Information
 Collier, Gary D. *Scribes Trained for the Kingdom: A Pre-Grammar for New Testament Greek as a Spiritual Discipline.* (A 10 Week Short-Course for English Bible Readers). The Dialogē Press, November 2019.

Contact Information
 The Dialogē Press
 452 W. Water Street, Box 121, Cloverdale, IN 46120
 Email: managingeditor@coffeewithpaul.com Website: BiblicalConversation.com

Version Date: Friday, November 1, 2019

Publisher's Cataloging-in-Publication Data

Names: Collier, Gary D., 1950-
Title: Scribes Trained for the Kingdom: A Pre-Grammar for New Testament Greek as a
 Spiritual Discipline / Gary D. Collier.
Description: Cloverdale, IN : The Dialogē Press, 2019. | Illustrations; 8 tables. |
Includes bibliographic references. | Summary: A 10 week short-course for English Bible
readers addressing the question: "Why Study New Testament Greek?"
Identifiers: LCCN 2019909949 | ISBN 9780998323077 (hbk.) | ISBN 9780998323084 (ebook)
Subjects: LCSH: Greek language, Biblical--Grammar. 2. Bible. N.T.—Language, style. I.
 Title. | BISAC: RELIGION / Biblical Reference / Language Study.
Classification: LCC PA817.C65 2019 (print) | LCC PA817 (ebook) | DDC 487'.4—dc22
LC record available at https://lccn.loc.gov/2019909949
Library of Congress Control Number:2019909949

For Michael Wilkinson

FOREWORD

Spiritual disciplines have always intrigued me, but Greek, not so much. The minimum requirement of Introduction to biblical languages, and the occasional use of an interlinear, were enough for me to skate through college without the "drudgery" of flashcards and grammar cramming. From there, I went directly into the ministry world and for thirty years have found myself with an increasingly large ministry schedule of opportunity and responsibility. During these busy years the lifelines of the spiritual disciplines have sustained me, but interest in, and attention to Greek languages escaped me.

Enter my friend, the author of this book, Gary Collier. Gary has taught Greek for the past thirty years. He is more passionate about the language in which Scripture was written than anyone I've ever met. His appreciation and excitement for Greek is contagious. His humble, practical, non-elitist, unpretentious demeanor allows students at any level to taste the value and beauty of the original languages. As he does this, he does not minimize the unyielding demands of language pursuit, but does promote and unveil the real possibility of learning.

Gary introduced me to Greek several years ago and has greatly enriched my understanding of Scripture and ministry. Having read several of his books, I was eager to see his perspective on **Greek as a Spiritual Discipline.** Imagine the benefits of wading around in the mind of God, in the language not only of the New Testament, but also of the Greek Old Testament (which most early Christians read and heard), and using it all the while as a spiritual discipline. I was intrigued the moment I saw the title.

Gary does not disappoint. He does a masterful job of inviting his readers onto the front porch of Greek studies and enticing them to step into its dwelling. He writes in such a way that those who do not consider themselves academics, or who have perhaps had bad Greek experiences, or have been intimidated by the prospect of language studies can take bite sized, confidence building, value adding steps toward understanding and using Greek. To make it even better he does this through what he considers a key verse in Matthew and he uses this passage not only to teach basic Greek and to showcase the value of understanding Greek, but also to set some benchmarks that increase our appreciation for the merging of language study and spiritual discipline. His discussion of spiritual disciplines alone is worthwhile, but combined with his expertise and love of New Testament Greek, this book provides a brief but exhilarating test drive of Greek as a spiritual discipline.

As a lifelong disciple and disciple maker, I continue to depend on the lifelines of spiritual discipline, but Dr. Collier has provided a whole new raft of benchmarks and nuances to assist me in my pursuits. I love this book. Like a trailer to a great movie, this will whet your appetite for the greater experience. This tool can help you move from not knowing Greek at all or "knowing just enough to be dangerous" to increasingly understanding more as you approach Greek as a spiritual discipline to interact with God and Scripture in your quest to be a "scribe trained for the kingdom, bringing out of your treasures both old and new."

Jeff Faull
Sr. Minister, Mt. Gilead Church
Mooresville, Indiana

Table of Contents

Foreword..5

Journaling..11

Chapter Format..11

Master List: The 7 Spiritual Benchmarks.......................13

1 A GREEK EXPERIENCE 15

Why Greek? 15
  Excitement 15
  Let's Be Honest 16
  Completely Honest... 18
  Consider the Spirit in You 19
Time for Greek: Alphabet 19
  Learn the Alphabet.. 19
  How to Write the Alphabet 21
  Discipline Yourself 22

2 A SPIRITUAL DISCIPLINE 23

Serving God 23
  It's Up to You 23
  Get Clear about Spiritual Disciplines.......................... 24
  Consider the Spirit in You 28
Time for Greek: Pronunciation (1).................................. 29
  Start Pronouncing 29
  Discipline Yourself 31

3 A TIME TO SOW 33

Expectations.. 33
  What Do You Expect? 33
  Answers to "Why?" 34
  Consider the Spirit in You 37
Time for Greek: Pronunciation (2)................................. 38
  Vocabulary 38
  Translate This... 38
  Discipline Yourself 38
  Translation Key 40

4 SCRIBES..**41**

   Spiritual Benchmark #1 41

      Guide Text: *41*

      Scribes *41*

      Consider the Spirit in You *43*

   Time for Greek: Verbs (1) 44

      Vocabulary *44*

      Greek Verbs--Basics *44*

      Translate This *46*

      Discipline Yourself *47*

      Translation Key *48*

5 TRAINED **49**

   Spiritual Benchmark #2 49

      Guide Text: *49*

      Trained *49*

      Consider the Spirit in You *53*

   Time for Greek: Verbs (2) 54

      Vocabulary *54*

      More on Greek Verbs *54*

      Translate This *55*

      Discipline Yourself *56*

      Translation Key *56*

6 KINGDOM OF HEAVEN **57**

   Spiritual Benchmark #3 57

      Guide Text: *57*

      Kingdom of Heaven *57*

      Consider the Spirit in You *63*

   Time for Greek: Nouns 64

      Vocabulary *64*

      Nouns *64*

      Translate This *68*

      Discipline Yourself *68*

      WARNING: *69*

      Translation Key *70*

7 HOUSEHOLD MANAGER **71**

   Spiritual Benchmark #4 71

      Guide Text: *71*

      Household Manager *71*

      Consider the Spirit in You *75*

Time for Greek: "The" 76
    Vocabulary 76
    24 Ways to Say "The" 76
    Translate This 81
    Discipline Yourself 81
    Translation Key 82
    Learn the Article by Heart 83

8 TREASURE **85**
  Spiritual Benchmark #5 85
    Guide Text: 85
    Treasure 85
    Consider the Spirit in You 88
  Time for Greek: Adjectives (1) 90
    Vocabulary 90
    Adjectives 90
    Translate This 93
    Discipline Yourself 93
    Translation Key 94

9 NEW **95**
  Spiritual Benchmark #6 95
    Guide Text: 95
    New 95
    Consider the Spirit in You 100
  Time for Greek: Adjectives (2) 101
    Vocabulary 101
    More about Adjectives 101
    Translate This 103
    Discipline Yourself 103
    Translation Key 104

10 OLD **105**
  Spiritual Benchmark #7 105
    Guide Text: 105
    Old 105
    Consider the Spirit in You 109
  Time for Greek: Next Steps & Resources 110
    Congratulations 110
    Next Steps 110
    Major Greek Tools & Resources 112
    Online Greek Helps 116

Discipline Yourself..*117*

APPENDIX **121**
  1. Vocabulary..122
  2. Resources Used or Quoted.....................................123
  3. Abbreviations..126

AUTHOR **130**

JOURNALING

Think about how the Spirit of God is at work inside of you at this very moment. That is what **"Consider the Spirit in You"** is all about (the very last subheading of every chapter before you get to "Time for Greek." See the Table of Contents.) This section is not about whether you feel harried or excited, happy or sad. It is, instead, challenging you to take up a personal journal, a notebook specifically for charting your progress each time you come to this section.

No one can *force* you to do this. Spiritual discipline cannot be forced and is not about coercion. You should do it on your own *because you long for spiritual discipline.*

CHAPTER FORMAT

As a *Pre-Grammar*, this book is intended as a prelude leading to New Testament (NT) Greek studies. (1) *It focuses on why* the pursuit of Greek as a spiritual discipline can be an exciting adventure that forever changes the way you read the Bible; and (2) *it gives you a taste* of the language — a kind of "jump start." Each chapter is divided into two sections:

1. **SPIRITUAL DISCIPLINE** (with various titles)
    The first section of each chapter is the primary focus of the book. It emphasizes and illustrates *why* the pursuit of NT Greek can be a *spiritual* discipline: a life-long encounter with biblical texts,[1] a *spiritual* journey.

    a. Chapters 1-3 briefly describe spiritual disciplines and why the pursuit of NT Greek belongs here.

    b. Chapters 4-10 lay out seven (7) *benchmarks,* one for each chapter. By looking at one specific text from the Gospel of Matthew (13:52), these chapters

---

[1] Both OT and NT. Remember, most of the earliest Christians, including all of the writers of NT documents, read their sacred texts primarily in Greek.

highlight the pursuit of NT Greek as *one way of serving God*: a truly *spiritual* discipline.

2. **TIME FOR GREEK** (always this title)
    The second section of each chapter offers *some very basic Greek, enough to give readers a taste for the language.* This is not a "shortcut" to learning Greek. (There is no such thing.) Here, a mere taste of Greek is offered at a light pace, a kind of "jump start" into the language, or maybe like a "sampler" in a restaurant. This small amount of the language is intended *to help you see the larger picture* as a way of serving God and to *whet your appetite* for taking the next step.

Warning: *If you focus only or even primarily on the Greek part of this book, you will entirely miss the point of the book.*

MASTER LIST:
THE 7 SPIRITUAL BENCHMARKS

Write the *Benchmarks* from Chapters 4-10.

1. _____

   _____

2. _____

   _____

3. _____

   _____

4. _____

   _____

5. _____

   _____

6. _____

   _____

7. _____

   _____

1
A Greek Experience

WHY GREEK?

I remember it as vividly as I see my computer screen right now. I had spent weeks poring over one Greek or Hebrew text after another: New Testament, Old Testament, Apocryphal and Pseudepigraphical books, Philo, Josephus, and Rabbinic texts. They were fascinating! I was trying to understand *why* the Apostle Paul, likely the earliest of all New Testament writers, made the argument he did in 1Corinthians 10:1-13.

EXCITEMENT

I had read all the English translations and tons of secondary literature on it (you know, all the stuff by one biblical scholar and another), and I had learned a great deal, but that was only a small thing. It is important to be "conversant" with what others say about a text, but it is incredibly shallow not to engage ancient texts firsthand, as if one-on-one with their authors. So, I read these texts over and over again, as if I was having an intense conversation with them. And on Tuesday morning, at 10:47 in the quiet of my southern California office, I laid my eyes—for the 49th time—on a simple Greek verb, "and they rose up," only this time it reached out and grabbed me, riveting my unblinking gaze so that months of work came suddenly into a bright light of crystal-clarity.

I'm not talking about remembering a vocabulary word. I'm talking about being overcome by what that ancient author was doing with that simple Greek verb in context. It is difficult to describe the rush of adrenaline and emotion that seized me—it was a joy that went well beyond any of the previous frustrations of not "getting it." For about 2 hours I was so overcome by excitement that I could not sit in a chair or stop pacing the floor.[2]

It sounds silly to anyone who has not experienced it. And when I have opened up to share this with others, some just laugh, or dismiss it as delusion or indigestion. But I know better. It was God!

Now by this I don't mean that God swooped down and gave me a revelation of "the one-and-only truth" never before understood by anyone else. In that sense I agree with the others, and I try never to blame God for what might turn out to be my own propensity towards hallucination. But I'm talking about something different. I refer to experiencing God in the deep conversations that were taking place within and among those biblical texts—an experience in which *insight* shakes the soul with the rigor of a 10 on the Richter scale! I speak not of "correct answers" so much as being allowed to participate in an ancient conversation, only now as if I were personally sitting at that table.

The point, here, is not that English-only readers of the Bible cannot experience the depths of God's wonder, for that wonder is not confined to any human language, whether English or Greek. The point is, rather, that the study of the Bible in its original languages can be exciting and can open doors that are not quite expected—if one can but catch that vision.

LET'S BE HONEST

The problem with my story is that it is not the one most people associate with Greek. And I would say that the study of Greek often gets a bum rap both in academic and church settings. Two or three stories will illustrate this problem.

First, during the past 30 years I have been privileged to teach what is commonly called Hellenistic Greek (which includes the language of the New Testament and related literature) in settings ranging from churches to seminaries and from adult Bible schools

---

[2] This eventually became Collier 1994 (Note: All resources quoted in this book are listed in this fashion. See Appendix "Resources Used or Quoted" for full reference.)

to universities. During that time, I have used a wide variety of beginning and advanced grammars, all aimed at giving students a thorough understanding of the language.

But by the time I arrived at Martin University in late 1996, I had become convinced of the need to develop a more practical approach to teaching this wonderful language to a wider audience than just "Bible majors." University Greek programs in general were necessarily demanding, and yet for years I had been bothered by the number of students who get nearly run over by Greek and who end up with a bad Greek experience.

When I say, "run over," I mean it. This extended all the way back to my first semester as a Greek student in which about 35 students had signed up to take Greek. By the end of the first year, only about ten of us remained. By the end of year two, about six. When I signed up for third year Greek, I found myself sitting in my professor's office—just the two of us. I loved the personal attention, but I wondered what had happened to everyone else. Unfortunately, this is not an uncommon experience in other programs around the country.

During the same period of time I often would run into those who had studied Greek in an academic setting and who had horror stories about what they almost universally call their "Greek Experience." Very often they described it as a kind of visit to a haunted house at Halloween, and in many cases they were left with lasting scars of failure, regret, or bitterness.

Since this was not the experience I had at all (or of many others), I kept asking why there was such an attrition rate? There are many reasons, of course: not everyone is required to take Greek, and not everyone has the time, or interest, or perhaps the facility for it. Some sit out for a year or more, only to return later; and not every teacher has the patience or energy some students need. In fact, some teachers, aiming only at the "best" students, seem to delight in blowing others out of the class with an elitist air that "Greek is only for the truly serious students."

My next two stories are more down to earth and illustrate that just the word "Greek" among some Christians can create a negative reaction. I remember sitting at a table with a Christian man who asked me what I taught in college. When I said, "biblical languages: Greek and Hebrew" he donned an immediate scowl and said, "So does your study of Grrrrreeeeeeeeek make you better than everyone else?" On another occasion, when I was teaching a class in a church, I handed out my own translation of the text we were studying and said, "This is an aid to use with your own Bible." One woman was incensed: "What gives you the right to change God's word!"

Such reactions have always intrigued me. How can anything that helps us understand the Bible be a bad thing? Yet, I suppose I understand some of the emotions. On the one hand, some feel the Bible is being attacked, and others feel they keep getting mugged by Greek-spouting Bible teachers or preachers who do not handle Greek very graciously. On the other hand, some have always wanted to learn some Greek, but they think it is beyond their reach.

COMPLETELY HONEST

This is why a new look is deserved.

If we are up front about it, learning Greek can be intimidating; it can take a lot of time and energy.

But if we are *totally* up front about it, the whole truth must be told and must not get left out: namely, *New Testament Greek is an engaging tool (which means it will help you engage the biblical text)* regardless of your "walk of life," and especially if you love the Bible and want more from it. It can encourage, inspire, engage, and challenge followers of Jesus as they seek to become what Jesus called *scribes trained for the Kingdom of Heaven.* (I will soon get to discussing this statement by Jesus.)

For me personally, I never feel closer to God than when I am walking around neck-deep in a biblical Greek text. And that's the truth, the whole truth, and nothing but the truth.[3]

---

[3] I would certainly make this statement about Greek, Hebrew, and Aramaic texts of the entire Bible. But more so Greek for me, since early believers in Christ

CONSIDER THE SPIRIT IN YOU

Take up your journal and write about how the Spirit of God is working on you at this very moment.

1. How much time do you spend in activities that encourage, build, and strengthen your spiritual life?

2. Do you believe that understanding the Bible on a deeper level could contribute to an enhanced spiritual life?

3. Does it make sense to you that a discipline of learning the language in which the NT was written could be a *spiritual* discipline, and not simply an academic one?

TIME FOR GREEK: ALPHABET

LEARN THE ALPHABET

Learn to say the alphabet aloud and to write it. You already know half of the 24 Greek letters. Everyone knows π|p. Also, the vowels and a few consonants look and sound like English.

α	ε	ι	ο	υ		β	δ	ζ	κ	π	ς	τ
a	e	i	o	u		b	d	z	k	p	s	t

A few hints:
1. It is helpful to learn the alphabet in groups of 5 letters at a time. See under the heading *Discipline Yourself* below.

2. Teach the alphabet to a child (of about any age. My daughter learned it age 2). It becomes a fun game and will likely encourage you to learn it better.

3. Some people like singing the alphabet to the English alphabet song. Personally, I don't recommend it because you will always depend on the tune, and it will slow you down later. But it is up to you.

---

publicly read from, quoted, and relied on the sacred texts translated into Greek. The "Bible" the earliest church used was primarily in Greek.

Minuscule:

α β γ δ ε ζ η θ ι κ λ μ ν ξ ο π ρ σ | ς τ υ φ χ ψ ω

a b g d e z ē th i k l m n x o p r s|s t u ph ch ps ō

Uncial:

Α Β Γ Δ Ε Ζ Η Θ Ι Κ Λ Μ Ν Χ Ο Π Ρ   Σ   Τ Υ Φ Χ Ψ Ω

α	alpha	a*	alms, father
β	beta	b	bet
γ	gamma	g	gamma ray
δ	delta	d	delta
ε	epsilon	e (short e)	episode, met
ζ	zeta	dz	kids
η	eta	ē (long e)	prey
θ	theta	th	thespian, think
ι	iota	i	pit, machine
κ	kappa	k	kaput
λ	lambda	l	lamb
μ	mu	m	man
ν	nu	n	nose
ξ	xi	x	box, books
ο	omicron	o (short o)	log, on**
π	pi	p	pan
ρ	rho	r	run, river
σ | ς	sigma	s	suns (medial & final) ***
τ	tau	t	time, tonsil
υ	upsilon	u	use (German ü)
φ	phi	ph	phantom, philosopher
χ	chi	ch	Christological (not champion)
ψ	psi	ps	lapse, oops
ω	omega	ō (long o)	note, rode

*Third column is *transliteration*: γραμματεύς | *grammateus*.

**Because of varied pronunciation systems and entrenched practices, the omicron gets pronounced in one of three distinct ways: *log*, *not*, or *note*. The first, *log*, is best for learning purposes because it distinguishes it from both an alpha and omega. Campbell 2015 192-208 has an extended discussion about Greek pronunciation.

***The sigma has two forms like so: ἐκκλησίας: medial and final sigma. Marks over Greek letters (accents and the like) come next lesson.

HOW TO WRITE THE ALPHABET

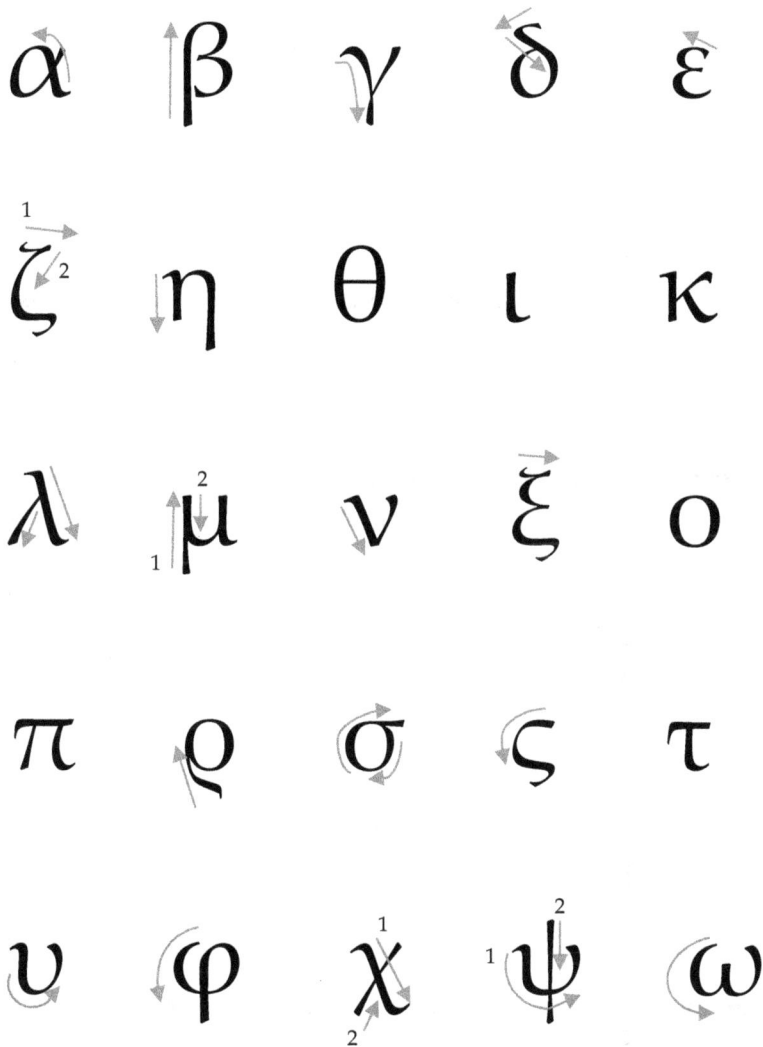

α   β   γ   δ   ε

ζ   η   θ   ι   κ

λ   μ   ν   ξ   ο

π   ρ   σ   ς   τ

υ   φ   χ   ψ   ω

DISCIPLINE YOURSELF

1. It is very important that you *learn the alphabet in order as soon as possible.* Ignore the upper case (uncial) letters. Learn the lower case (minuscule) letters.

2. Speak the alphabet out loud in order. Learn it in blocks: either (a) all at once, or perhaps (b) on successive days.

3. Copy this chart or use blank paper to practice writing the alphabet.

1 (Monday)	α a	β b	γ g	δ d	ε e
2 (Tuesday)	ζ d z	η ē	θ t h	ι i	κ k
3 (Wednesday)	λ l	μ m	ν n	ξ x	o o
4 (Thursday)	π p	ϱ r	σ s	ς s*	τ t
5 (Friday)	υ u	φ p h	χ c h	ψ p s	ω ō

*Do not say sigma twice, but mentally note both forms.

22

2
A Spiritual Discipline

SERVING GOD

I support the notion that Greek is for serious students. This is why I have come to view the study of biblical languages as a *spiritual discipline*—a journey that leads us before God in humility and fills us with great expectation. I came to this realization the more I started "hanging around" in the hallowed halls, not of school, but of Greek biblical texts.

IT'S UP TO YOU

I have more to say on this, but I hasten to say that I do not support an elitist attitude about Greek. One does not need to be a published Greek scholar to benefit from the study of Greek any more than one needs to be a gourmet cook to benefit from eating. In fact, eating for the sake of eating might be a bad thing, as Greek for its own sake might be detrimental to spirituality.

That said and kept firmly in mind, the study of ancient Greek approached expectantly and humbly, with passion and diligence (it's up to you), can be a breathtaking source of spiritual nurture. Just as spirituality may be pursued through classical disciplines, like prayer and fasting, the focused and careful study of the New Testament in the language it was written can open a window of fresh air for enlivened spirituality. It is not that understanding Greek participles somehow brings on the Holy Spirit (heartburn, maybe), it is rather that being able to gaze intently at a paragraph by Paul or John in the language it was actually written somehow opens windows in our hearts and souls. It helps us gain insight and even sympathy with those authors and their messages that no reading of any English text is able to give us. In a way, it is sometimes like the difference between reading a book and then watching the movie. The movie might be great, but the book still has more to it.

The study of biblical Greek won't make us super-Christians to dazzle our friends. It is not a badge to wear, or a cause for unruly pride. Rather, we pursue it as *one way of serving God* that our hearts might receive the messages and insights of the ancient authors whom we say we respect and follow.

GET CLEAR ABOUT SPIRITUAL DISCIPLINES

General Approaches

So, what is a spiritual discipline? Although not a definition per se, some great writers have written on the central focus of spiritual quests:

> "The detachment from the confusion all around us is in order to have a richer attachment to God. Christian meditation leads us to the inner wholeness necessary to give ourselves to God freely." (Richard Foster, *Celebration of Discipline*)[4]

> "Meditation has no point and no reality unless it is firmly rooted in *life*." (Thomas Merton, *Contemplative Prayer*)[5]

> "By means of the imagination, we confine our mind within the mystery on which we meditate, that it may not ramble to and fro..." (Francis de Sales, *Introduction to the Devout Life*)[6]

Not one of these statements was made about the study of the NT in its ancient Greek language. But all of them apply, if we have eyes to see and a heart for adventure.

"Discipline" in English Translations

It is interesting to note that despite all of the attention given to spiritual disciplines, no biblical text comes right out with "and here are the five, or seven, or thirteen spiritual disciplines you must follow." Students of the Bible should understand from the outset that the pursuit of "spiritual disciplines" is a theological

---

[4] Foster 1988, 21.

[5] Merton 1969, 39.

[6] de Sales, n.d. end of chapter 4.

and traditional quest, not one based on any given text. In fact, the following chart is quite instructive showing the number of times the word "discipline" occurs in the listed English translations:

	1	2	3	4		5
	OT	NT	Apoc	Total		All
KJV	1	0	0	**1**		**1**
ASV	0	1	0	**1**		**1**
NJB	18	2	11	**31**		**34**
NASB	25	12	--	**37**		**50**
NIV	29	6	--	**35**		**51**
RSV	16	7	15	**38**		**53**
NAB	24	7	16	**47**		**57**
NET	32	10	--	**42**		**58**
ESV	35	8	--	**43**		**60**
NRSV	28	11	18	**57**		**81**
NETS (LXX)**	53	---	23	**76**		**103**

*Columns 1-4 show only the form "discipline."
Column 5 shows all forms including "discipline (-s, -ed, -ing)."
This chart is arranged by frequency in column 5.
**LXX stands for the Greek OT, commonly called the Septuagint.

Table 1

As a matter of fact, the phrase "spiritual discipline"[7] never occurs in any translation of the Bible and we should rightly draw from this that there was no concern in any biblical text for any kind of institutionalized approach called by such a name.

Even so, biblical texts clearly encourage followers of Jesus to seek and submit to God's Spirit. Such things as singing, praying, and fasting had long been part of Jewish life, both private and corporate. The reading of the sacred texts was considered a necessary and expected part of following, worshipping, and obeying the One God of Israel. All of this was passed along to the earliest Christ-followers.

---

[7] We will give attention to the Greek word for discipline as we proceed.

In the best of Jewish and Christian teaching, such activities were never seen as an end in themselves.[8] It was never taught that if you would simply attend Temple, or sacrifice, or sing, or pray, or hear sacred texts that you could then say, "I am now righteous! I am now spiritual!" (It might be true that people tend down this road, but that was never what Jewish or Christian teaching was about.) This would be like saying, "Because I eat, I am healthy!" Just because you like to eat does not make you healthy; just because you like to sing (or read Greek!) does not make you spiritual. The activities above, whether Jewish or Christian, were never ends in themselves.

Identifying Spiritual Disciplines

So, what is it that makes singing, or praying, or read texts, or anything else a *spiritual* discipline? Are there characteristics that help you to identify them? This is a debated question: whether a spiritual discipline has to be derived from the Bible or not; whether the Bible *defines and delimits* spiritual disciplines or merely *attests* that such activities may exist.

I belong more to the second opinion, but an example from the first is the highly respected author and teacher Don Whitney (author of *Spiritual Disciplines for the Christian Life*[9] and professor of Biblical Spirituality and Associate Dean of the School of Theology at The Southern Baptist Theological Seminary in Louisville.). Giving an online interview[10] on the podcast "Desiring God" (founded by John Piper), Whitney described spiritual disciplines as having six characteristics:

1. They are derived from the Bible (both personal and corporate spiritual disciplines).

---

[8] Despite the fact that many Jews, like many Christians still, turned the message of God into a kind of legalistic "I've earned your grace now!," that was never a part of OT teaching. And this despite the fact that many Christians to this day think (and say) "The OT was law, the NT grace." This is a gross misunderstanding of both OT and NT texts that I will not take the time here to demolish.

[9] Whitney 2014

[10] Whitney 2015

2. They are activities (not just attitudes).

3. They are practices taught or modeled in the Bible itself.

4. They are limited to those found (listed or talked about) in the Bible, which are "sufficient for knowing and experiencing God and for growing in Christlikeness".

5. They are derived from the gospel, not divorced from the gospel.

6. They are "the means to godliness," not an end in themselves.

This is, of course, a helpful effort for giving some definition to the phrase "spiritual discipline." However, whether the various biblical texts attempt to *establish and define* spiritual disciplines can be challenged. Perhaps it is better to say that biblical texts *attest to* and *allow for* them without any attempt to name anything like a list of them, or to limit them, or to set up boundaries for them. Although I appreciate the list above, and although I suppose that one might call such a list "biblically related disciplines," I personally find it too confining.

In a real sense, this is like talking about whether the Bible *defines and limits* spiritual gifts to only 21, or whether said gifts listed in various scattered texts for different reasons (mostly Pauline: Rom 12:6-8; 1Cor 12:8-10, 28-30; Eph 4:11; 1Pet 4:11) *illustrate* the ways in which God gifts his people in specific circumstances.

In both examples (disciplines and gifts), the second reading is preferable. Furthermore, gifts are specifically called by this name, whereas disciplines are not. (As noted, these are theologically derived and named.) Contextual readings of these texts show them to be addressing specific situations, not attempting to ensure that a group of disciplines get labeled as such.

Drawing Close to God

Christian spiritual disciplines, then, are primarily about one thing: walking in the presence of God. This is not about isolating or identifying a "correct set of activities" that biblical texts attempt to define; instead, this includes *activities and practices of all kinds that draw us into the presence of God through his Spirit.* Some of these are named in biblical texts (prayer, fasting, etc.), and others just show up in the lives of people (like Joseph, David, Deborah, Elijah, and Ezra; or like Joseph and Mary, Barnabas, Peter, Paul, Nicodemus, Phoebe, Dorcas, Mary Magdalene, and others).

In our case, I am specifically suggesting that biblical Greek be approached as a *spiritual* discipline (instead of merely as an *academic* discipline), a discipline of the mind and heart to help us focus on the message—the very words—of God. Any other approach to this language is outside of what we are after in this course.

CONSIDER THE SPIRIT IN YOU

After spending some time contemplating, **take up your journal and write** about the following questions:

1. In what ways does this lesson challenge or support your views on *spiritual disciplines* up to now?

2. Give some thought to the question whether the various biblical texts attempt to *establish and define* spiritual disciplines (perhaps as commands), or they *attest to* and *allow for* such discipline without any attempt to name anything like a list of them. What do you think about this?

TIME FOR GREEK: PRONUNCIATION (1)

START PRONOUNCING

Vowels: Vowels are the same as in English, except there are two o's and two e's:

α

ε (short e = *met*)   η (long e = *prey*)

ι

ο (short o = *log, on*)[11]   ω (long o = *omega*)

υ

Diphthongs: a combination of two vowels resulting in *a new vowel sound* and treated as if they were only one vowel. The final letter is always an ι or an υ. The main ones are as follows:

αι	aisle	αυ	**cow** (cf. German "**au**to" = car)
ει	eight	ευ	feud
οι	oil	ου	group
υι	suite		

Other combinations of vowels are not diphthongs:
e.g., ἐθ**εα**σάμεθα = ἐ / θ**ε** / **α** / σά / με / θα

Iota Subscript: a small iota written under three Greek vowels:
ᾳ ῃ ῳ (transliterated as $\bar{a}_i$, $\bar{e}_i$, and $\bar{o}_i$). Pronounce each letter as if there were no iota.

Note:

Transliterate: λόγος = *logos* (letter by letter).

Translate: λόγος = "word" (meaning of the word).

---

[11] The terms *short* and *long* here refer to Greek accent rules (which we will not discuss), not to how English vowels are pronounced. As mentioned above, it is likely best to pronounce the omicron as *log*, rather than either *not* or *note* so as to distinguish it from both the alpha and the omega.

Breathing Marks: An "h" sound is designated this way:
ἑν =hen (called a rough breathing); ἐν = en (called a smooth breathing). Note the direction of the mark above the vowel.

Accents: Three accents:

acute	= λόγος
circumflex	= ἀρχῆ
grave	= τὸν

Don't fret over the names. For our purposes, if a syllable has an accent, emphasize it. That's it!

(English has accents, too, just not written—for example, the old joke, "Putting the emphAsis on the wrong syllAble.")

Punctuation:

Comma	,
Period	.
Colon/Semicolon	·
Question mark	;

Syllables: Break each word into syllables: When you sit down to a meal, you don't eat the whole meal in one bite. When pronouncing Greek words, take one bite at a time. Divide them into syllables and pronounce one syllable at a time.

Here's the key:

*One vowel **sound** per syllable.*

This means a diphthong (αι, ει, οι etc.) is only one vowel sound. Divide consonants where it seems to make sense (as in English) based on vowel sounds.

Example: γραμματεὺς = γραμ / μα / τεὺς
μαθητευθεὶς = μα / θη / τευ / θεὶς

Always pronounce Greek words aloud (so you can hear them). At first, focus on *only one syllable at a time*. Don't worry about how fast you are.

Special Notes: It is helpful to know the following:

Name	Greek Letter	Translit- eration	Special Notes
gamma	γ	g	gg, kg, and xg = ng—ἄγγελος = *angelos*
sigma	σ or ς	s	Both = s. E.g., πίσις = *pistis* ("faith")
upsilon	υ	u	For simplicity, υ is always u, instead of y.
chi	χ	ch	As in <u>Ch</u>rist, never as in <u>ch</u>urch.

DISCIPLINE YOURSELF

Every chapter has this Greek section *(Discipline Yourself)* near the end. It is important that *discipline is bathed in prayer.* Even though this is Greek, keep your focus on *spiritual* discipline.

Obviously, *spiritual* does not mean lazy, irresponsible, or shoddy work. If anything, *spiritual implies excellence.* And if you are one of those people who thinks the Spirit will give you all the answers you need (while you do nothing at all), then you will soon be saying that the Spirit is telling you that Greek is not worth your time! It is possible that you will not enjoy learning some Greek — just don't blame it on the Holy Spirit of God.

Now for this week:

1. **Keep saying and writing the Alphabet.** Focus on solidifying it this week. Some will learn this quickly. Some won't. To help you get comfortable with the alphabet, make copies of the next page and practice writing it. Be sure to say it aloud, in order, and often.

2. **Don't lie to yourself.** Someone always says: *"Well, I recognize the different letters, so I don't really need to learn them in order."* Hear what the Spirit says: "I wish you were either cold or hot!" Here's a mystery once hidden but now revealed: if you don't know the alphabet in order, you can't even look up a word in the dictionary!

Learn the alphabet in order! Say it aloud! Practice writing it!

α   β   γ   δ   ε

—— —— —— —— ——

—— —— —— —— ——

—— —— —— —— ——

ζ   η   θ   ι   κ

—— —— —— —— ——

—— —— —— —— ——

—— —— —— —— ——

λ   μ   ν   ξ   ο

—— —— —— —— ——

—— —— —— —— ——

—— —— —— —— ——

π   ϱ   σ   ς   τ

—— —— —— —— ——

—— —— —— —— ——

—— —— —— —— ——

υ   φ   χ   ψ   ω

—— —— —— —— ——

—— —— —— —— ——

—— —— —— —— ——

3
A Time to Sow

EXPECTATIONS

"A sower went out to sow." There was a path, some rocks, some thorns, and some rich, fertile soil. So begins the greatest collection of Jesus' parables in the NT (Matthew 13, the single best description of students there ever was). This is followed by seven more parables: "The Kingdom of Heaven is like . . ." At the end (13:52) is a scribe—a student of the scriptures and of Jesus' teachings. And that scribe (like the sower) is there for only one reason: *to scribe!*

The question is: *What are you doing here?* You know those stories in English. In this book, you'll take a close look at the last one (the scribe), only this time from Greek. You have the center seat. The story is about you. The question is: *Are you ready?*

WHAT DO YOU EXPECT?

What are you expecting to get from an introduction to the study of NT Greek as a spiritual discipline? To help you with this, here are some things you can expect:

> You can expect the same you get by eating right, exercising, and getting plenty of rest: *However, this will not only feed and sustain you, it will create in you a desire for more!*

> You can expect to enhance and even energize your praying and reading of biblical texts. Think about it. *This will have you walking around in the words of God![12] It can refresh your heart, soul, and mind! And when it is approached as a spiritual quest, marvelous things can happen!*

---

[12] I so much want to add: "duh!"

Even if you have no interest in becoming a Greek scholar (and most who read this book won't have that goal), if you approach it steadily as a spiritual walk, a pursuit of biblical Greek as a form of Bible study is an activity and ongoing practice that can discipline you in some powerful ways:

1. It can encourage you to focus and train your mind to think in ancient Christian categories, not just in terms of current Christian fads and whims;

2. It can help you read and understand our wide variety of English Bibles better;

3. It can enable you to understand the processes of ancient biblical cultures, bringing insight into biblical concepts beyond what English alone can provide;

4. It can cause you to broaden yourself and gain theological perspective;

5. It can bring you insight into biblical words and texts that you will never gain from English translations;

6. It can promote an informed view of the origin, nature, and current status of the Holy Writings produced by and for Christianity; and

7. It can provide a foundation for every type of ministry interest.

The study of biblical Greek as a spiritual discipline just makes sense. It's not that simply knowing the language makes you more spiritual, it's that spiritual goals in pursuit of the language can be incredibly rewarding.

ANSWERS TO "WHY?"

Why This Course?

Why? Because this course wants to help you have a spiritual "Aha" life! (Not just an aha moment.) As an English Bible reader, you hopefully will see how biblical Greek can help you walk with God!

If you can leave this course seeing how the study of biblical Greek could be approached as a *spiritual* discipline, then we will have accomplished something important together. During this time, you'll also learn a few very basic Greek skills—but only enough to whet your appetite:

1. How to recite the Greek Alphabet in order.

2. How to pronounce any Greek word or group of words in the Greek NT.

3. About 30 words (all the words in Mt 13:52 plus a few)

4. Some very basic things about a Greek Interlinear text.

5. Some very basic things about Greek lexicons, concordances, word study books, and computer tools. Mostly, you will watch me use them.

6. Some basics about using various English translations.

The burden of this course is light and very doable. You should plan to spend about 30-60 minutes every day (5 or 6 days each week). You will learn some Greek, but that will not be our emphasis. It will rather be on why a study of Greek can ignite a spiritual fire in those who want to be what Jesus called *scribes trained for the Kingdom of Heaven.*

Why This Text?

We will spend seven weeks (a perfect 7) looking at only one verse from a saying of Jesus that is found only in **Mt 13:52**:

ὁ δὲ εἶπεν αὐτοῖς· διὰ τοῦτο πᾶς γραμματεὺς μαθητευθεὶς
And he said to them: "Because of this, every scribe who has been trained

τῇ βασιλείᾳ τῶν οὐρανῶν ὅμοιός ἐστιν ἀνθρώπῳ οἰκοδεσπότῃ,
for the Kingdom of Heaven   is like   a master of a household,

ὅστις ἐκβάλλει ἐκ τοῦ θησαυροῦ αὐτοῦ καινὰ καὶ παλαιά.
who   brings out from   his treasure   new things and old.

We'll look at every part of this verse.

Why? Because this is a powerful text. It is ideal to demonstrate Greek as a spiritual discipline. This Greek text

1. presents *Jesus speaking* to his disciples in Matthew's telling of the Jesus-story;

2. is about being *trained, discipled, or taught* (the aspect of *discipline* that speaks of learning);[13]

3. introduces the notion of a *treasure house* or room in which disciples must *evaluate* alternatives and options;

4. will help illustrate all seven of the *Spiritual Benchmarks* of this class.

By focusing on a specific, small NT text, along with a very few Greek details, the study of biblical Greek is both slowed down to a manageable pace and focused on issues relating to Jesus' call to discipleship. This text contains about 25 words, and we will learn them (and a few others) as a way of getting into the subject. In this way, our topic will be contextualized.

Why This Structure?

Why? Because it gets right to the point and keeps us on track! Every lesson will contain the following elements:

1. A main focus on a new *Spiritual Benchmark*. This will be some aspect of Greek as a spiritual discipline, always drawing from Mt 13:52;

2. A brief look at a few basic Greek features;

3. The alphabet and then about 3-5 new vocabulary words per lesson and how to pronounce them out loud;

4. A sustained look at an interlinear text (in every class) of our main NT text; and

5. A demonstration of Greek as a spiritual discipline in the use of a few basic Greek tools.

---

[13] This is μαθητεύω/*mathēteuō*, "to discipline oneself as a learner or adherent." Another is παιδεύω/*paideuō*, "to instruct, correct, discipline."

Time to Sow

It's time to sow. This course is not complicated, and it is very sharply focused. It is more about *why* than anything else. It has a very practical aim so that you can have a positive and useful experience.

CONSIDER THE SPIRIT IN YOU

Please slow down for a moment. Become aware of your surroundings, of your breathing, of your heartbeat, of your state of mind. Relax a moment.

Now **take up your journal and write** about the following questions:

1. What are you expecting or anticipating from this class? Or better: What do you *hope* to get from this class?

2. Describe why you think your *spiritual life* might benefit from time spent in this class.

3. When you think about the fact that you are, right now, taking your first steps on a new path for *learning a new skill* that might forever change your Bible reading life, how does that make you feel?

TIME FOR GREEK: PRONUNCIATION (2)

VOCABULARY

Always memorize all vocabulary words in each lesson.

καί	"and"
ἔστιν	"he (or she or it) is"
λόγος	"word, message"
ὁ δὲ εἶπεν	"and he said"
γραμματεύς	"scribe, lawyer, expert in the law" (cf. English *grammatical*)
ἄνθρωπος	"a person, a human, a man" (noun)

TRANSLATE THIS

1. ἔστιν γραμματεύς.

2. γραμματεύς ἔστιν ἄνθρωπος.

(A Translation Key is always at chapter end.)

DISCIPLINE YOURSELF

Keep pronouncing words. To help you, here are two texts for practice. First, look at **Mt 5:30**. It is a *pangram* (i.e., has all the letters of the alphabet). Practice writing the letters, and then pronounce each word.

Do not try to translate any of this. It is too early for that.

καὶ εἰ ἡ δεξιά σου χεὶρ σκανδαλίζει σε,

ἔκκοψον αὐτὴν καὶ βάλε ἀπὸ σοῦ·

συμφέρει γάρ σοι ἵνα ἀπόληται ἓν τῶν

μελῶν σου καὶ μὴ ὅλον τὸ σῶμά σου

εἰς γέενναν ἀπέλθῃ

Second, look at **Mt 13:52**, our main text. We'll be looking at this text throughout the rest of this course. As with the previous text, practice writing the letters, and then pronounce each word. Do not give any concern for what these words mean. It is too early for that.

ὁ δὲ εἶπεν αὐτοῖς· διὰ τοῦτο πᾶς

γραμματεὺς μαθητευθεὶς τῇ βασιλείᾳ

τῶν οὐρανῶν ὅμοιός ἐστιν ἀνθρώπῳ

οἰκοδεσπότῃ, ὅστις ἐκβάλλει ἐκ τοῦ

θησαυροῦ αὐτοῦ καινὰ καὶ παλαιά.

TRANSLATION KEY

(for the sentences two pages up)

This is a fairly simple exercise; just take the words in order.

1. ἔστιν γραμματεύς.
   "he is   a scribe."

   ἔστιν is a verb that means *"he/she/it* is";
       Unlike English, all Greek verbs have built-in subjects.
       Context tells you which pronoun is needed.
       Since there is no context here, the subject could be *"he, she,* or *it"*

   γραμματεύς is a predicate nominative here (not the subject).

2. γραμματεύς ἔστιν ἄνθρωπος.
   "A scribe (he) is a person (a man)."

   γραμματεύς is now the subject = " A **scribe** (he) **is a person.**"

   ἔστιν This time, the "he/she/it" in the verb is taken over by the noun
       nom case subject "scribe." Hence the "he/she/it" is not needed in
       translation.

   ἄνθρωπος is now the predicate nominative.

4
Scribes

The study of NT Greek can . . .
make you a more disciplined student of the Bible.

GUIDE TEXT:

ὁ δὲ εἶπεν αὐτοῖς· διὰ τοῦτο **πᾶς γραμματεὺς** μαθητευθεὶς
And he said to them: "Because of this, **every scribe** who has been trained

τῇ βασιλείᾳ τῶν οὐρανῶν ὅμοιός ἐστιν ἀνθρώπῳ οἰκοδεσπότῃ,
for the Kingdom of Heaven   is like   a master of a household,

ὅστις ἐκβάλλει ἐκ τοῦ θησαυροῦ αὐτοῦ καινὰ   καὶ   παλαιά.
who   brings out from   the treasure   of him new things and   old.

SCRIBES

Quite honestly, the above text in Matthew often gets treated by readers as a throw-away line. However, it follows a question by Jesus: "Do you understand [the above parables I just told you]?" And they say, "Yes." Then he replies (above), and you can almost see the disciples looking at each other nervously, like "What'd he say?"

However, in Matthew's story of Jesus, this is no throw away line or clever "gotcha" moment. And it is not just an event that took place. This eighth parable is the dénouement, the grand finale, the exclamation point put on all of chapter 13—all eight parables. And if we don't get this one, we likely don't *understand* (a key word in this chapter)[14] much else.

---

[14] See Kingsbury 1995, 376.

The basic point? If you've been trained as a Jesus-follower, you understand how to interpret the old (traditions and teachings) through the new (Jesus' teachings).

It's not *quite* that simple. So, here we get our first taste of why Greek can be extremely helpful for understanding what is going on English translations of this verse. For example:

"scribe": KJV, ASV, RSV, NRS, NJB, ESV, NAS, NAB[15]

"teacher/expert in the law": NIV, NET, CSB17

It is not simply that they both mean the same things. The question is about whether this term γραμματεὺς | *grammateus* must refer to Jewish lawyers or (in Matthew) has a special sense for the followers of Jesus like "Christian scribes."[16] To see this clearly, look at the difference in the CSB and CSB17:

CSB   "every **student of Scripture** instructed in the kingdom of heaven"

CSB17 "every **teacher of the law** who has become a disciple in the kingdom of heaven"[17]

This means the translators changed their minds from the first to the second, or they were different translators. In the first, "scribe" was clearly understood as metaphorically applying to all followers of Jesus; in the second, the focus seems to be more on lawyers at that time who came to Jesus.

Also note this. Very important! Just to look up the word in a dictionary may not be enough. If this word is a special word in Matthew, used to imply something else, then a generic dictionary definition won't do at all. It might even obscure what is going on in this place.

---

[15] See list of English Translations in the Appendix.

[16] Biblical scholars get into these kinds of things. See Keener 2010, 393 et al; D&A 2004, 697. I will resist that temptation here for the sake of the nature and aim of this book.

[17] CSB was published in 2004 as the *Holman Christian Standard Bible*; it was revised in 2017 as simply the *Christian Standard Bible* (CSB17).

To explore this, we would do a word study on γραμματεὺς | *grammateus* and compare all uses. This sounds like a huge task, but it does not have to be. In fact, I just now did it, and it took 2.3 seconds. This word has a contextually defined usage in Matthew that points to Jesus' disciples as his trained scribes. As Jesus is the new and better Moses in Matthew, so his disciples are to be the new and better scribes.

So, it may be technically correct to translate this either as "scribe" or "teacher of the law," but in Mt 13:52, this is apparently pointing to what is supposed to take place in the community of Jesus-followers: they are supposed to know how to interpret the old in light of the new. This implies a lot of deep learning (training). It is not an automatic light-switch that gets flipped on when someone becomes a follower. Scribes trained for the kingdom are Jesus-followers who understand their important role with the scriptures.

Already, just by knowing a bit of Greek and using it to understand a spiritual truth, we see that *the study of NT Greek can make us more **disciplined** students of our ancient scriptures:* more disciplined in our questions, in the way we search for answers, and in the way we handle texts. No longer will we be satisfied with the common statement: "All the translations simply say the same things, just in different words." Not always they don't! Sometimes the differences matter! Scribes trained for the Kingdom want more. Using Greek to search for spiritual truth can be very helpful.

CONSIDER THE SPIRIT IN YOU

Before moving on, please **take up your journal and write**:

1. From this chapter, in what sense would you consider yourself *a scribe*? Or not?

2. Looking back across this lesson to *Spiritual Benchmark #1*, how does the prospect of your being a *scribe for the Kingdom of heaven* impact you? What do you think that means in your case?

TIME FOR GREEK: VERBS (1)

VOCABULARY

ἐκ	"out, out of, from" (preposition)
ἐκβάλλω	"I cast out, I bring out"
λύω	"I loose, release, set free"
μαθητεύω	"I disciple, teach, train, school." μαθητευθεὶς is a participle form and means "having discipled, etc."

GREEK VERBS--BASICS

How Verbs Work

Both English and Greek verbs have *tense*, *voice*, and *mood*. If you have a good grasp of grammar, this will make immediate sense. However, many English-speaking people don't have a good grasp of grammar. In any case, just look this over and don't try to memorize anything. (Don't fret the detail.) It is a table designed to help you say, "Oh, I get it!"

Tense:

Present	= general or continuing action in the present	"I baptize"
Future	= future action	"I will baptize"
Perfect	= completed action w/continuing results	"I have baptized"
Imperfect	= continuing action in the past	"I was baptizing"
Aorist	= general past, no indication of continuance	"I baptized"
Pluperfect	= past completed action	"I had baptized"

Voice:

Active	= denotes the subject as acting	"I baptize"
Middle	= the subject as reflexive or acting upon itself	"I baptize myself"
Passive	= the subject as being acted upon	"I am being baptized"

Mood:

Indicative	= denotes a statement or assertion	"I baptize"
Subjunctive	= possibility	"I might baptize"
Imperative	= command or request	"Baptize!"
Optative	= wish	"May I baptize"

Table 2

How English Verbs Are Built

On the next page, I'll start with English to show that you already are accustomed to certain principles about how verbs are built. I'll talk about "flags."

Flags: In English, verbs have certain properties (*flags*) that indicate how they are to be understood.

> The package *will arrive* tomorrow.
> The package *arrived* yesterday.
> The package *might arrive* this afternoon.

You know how to understand these sentences because you understand the *flags* with the verbs.

> <u>will</u> arrive = future
> arriv<u>ed</u> = past
> <u>might</u> arrive = possibility

How Greek Verbs Are Built

Like English, Greek verbs also have *flags*.

Unlike English, the Greek verb also has *number* and *person* built into the form of the verb.

Number	Singular	Plural
Person	I, you, he/she/it	we, you, they

English does this by placing a pronoun or other subject *before* the verb, "I take, you take, she takes, etc.).

But Greek does this by attaching *endings* on the verb. Greek places a "*flag*" on the end of each verb to show the person and number of the verb: λύ (*release*) + ω (*I*) = λύω (*I release*).

If English verbs attached the pronoun at the end of the verb, they would look something like this:

45

Singular	Plural
take*i*	take*we*
take*you*	take*youall*
take*he*, takes*he*, take*it*	take*they*

In other words, the same <u>flags</u> are still there, just in a different place. This is exactly what Greek does. Look at the following two charts:

The Verb λύω—"I release, I loose"

	Singular				Plural			
	Stem	+Ending	Word	Translation	Stem	+Ending	Word	Translation
1st	λυ	-ω	λύω	*I loose*	λυ	-ομεν	λύομεν	we loose
2nd	λυ	-εις	λύεις	*you loose*	λυ	-ετε	λύετε	ya'll loose
3rd	λυ	-ει	λύει	*he, she, it looses*	λυ	-ουσι	λύουσι	they loose

Table 3

What Should You Get out of This?

You should get the basic principle of verb formation: namely, **English and Greek verbs both have <u>flags</u>; they just put them in different places.** It *also* means that **all verbs have built-in subjects.** So, you can *always* tell if it is "I loose" or "he looses" etc. [Don't memorize the above chart, just understand the principle.]

TRANSLATE THIS

1. λύω, ἐκβάλλω, καὶ μαθητεύω.

2. λύεις καὶ ἐκβάλλομεν.

3. ἐκβάλλουσι καὶ μαθητεύομεν.

Discipline Yourself

This lesson has been a bare introduction to Greek verbs, and it is highly simplified. One step at a time.

1. Pray to God about yourself as a **scribe** being trained.

2. Review **the Greek section** until you understanding the principle it is trying to get across. Write down any lingering questions.

3. Review the **alphabet** at least once a day. Your goal is to learn it extremely well so you can say it fast. If you have trouble with it, teach it to a child. That child will then help you learn it.

4. Review all of your **vocabulary** every day.

5. **Read aloud:** As you have time, work on word pronunciation from the following text. Always pronounce the words aloud (don't try to translate):

   1. ὁ δὲ εἶπεν αὐτοῖς·διὰ τοῦτο πᾶς

   2. γραμματεὺς μαθητευθεὶς τῇ βασιλείᾳ

   3. τῶν οὐρανῶν ὅμοιός ἐστιν ἀνθρώπῳ

   4. οἰκοδεσπότῃ, ὅστις ἐκβάλλει ἐκ τοῦ

   5. θησαυροῦ αὐτοῦ καινὰ καὶ παλαιά.

TRANSLATION KEY

(for the sentences two pages up)

1. *"I loose, I bring out, I train."*
   (or) *"I set free, I cast out, I disciple."*
   λύω, ἐκβάλλω, καὶ μαθητεύω
   Remember, Greek verbs always contain a subject, and you find it in the verb endings. All of these verb endings are 1st sg. "I . . . "

2. *"You (sg) set free and we bring out."*
   (or) *"You (sg) release and we cast out."*
   Always look at the verb endings.
   λύεις 2nd sg = "you loose" or "you set free"
   ἐκβάλλομεν 1st pl = "we bring out" or "we cast out"

3. *"They cast out and we train."*
   (or) *"They bring out and we disciple."*
   ἐκβάλλουσι 3rd pl = "they bring out/cast out"
   μαθητεύομεν 1st pl = "we disciple/train"

5
Trained

SPIRITUAL BENCHMARK #2

The study of NT Greek can . . .
open up a new world of understanding.

GUIDE TEXT:

ὁ δὲ εἶπεν αὐτοῖς· διὰ τοῦτο πᾶς γραμματεὺς **μαθητευθεὶς**
And he said to them: "Because of this, every scribe who **has been trained**

τῇ βασιλείᾳ τῶν οὐρανῶν ὅμοιός ἐστιν ἀνθρώπῳ οἰκοδεσπότῃ,
for the Kingdom of Heaven   is like   a master of a household,

ὅστις ἐκβάλλει ἐκ τοῦ θησαυροῦ αὐτοῦ καινὰ   καὶ   παλαιά.
who   brings out from   the treasure   of him new things and   old.

TRAINED

Our emphasis in this chapter is that a life-long study of NT
Greek can open up a new world of understanding. It certainly
will not suddenly happen in this short chapter. But you should
mark it down as a principle that a sustained effort to this can be
rewarding for your spiritual vision.

Schooled/Discipled/Trained

Let's consider, for example, what it means to be "schooled"
for the Kingdom in Mt 13:52. English translations give at least 4
options:

"become a disciple *of* or *in* the K" (ASV, NIV, NJB, NAS, CSB17)

"instructed *in* the K" (KJV, SCB, NAB)

 "trained *for* the K" (RSV, NRS, ESV)

"trained as a disciple *for* the K" (CEB)

Even from just a simple standpoint, these obviously don't all mean the same things. We might certainly discuss the different implications of the prepositions: *of, in, for.* Even the similar verbs might imply different things. And the phrases as a whole: To *become a disciple of* or *in* or *to be instructed in* the Kingdom—all seem to imply a less active nuance than *trained for the Kingdom,* which comes across as almost activist or revolutionary for the sake of the Kingdom.

Which One is Right?

Which one is "right"? Or is that the best question? Fact is, all four of these are possible. Maybe we should note that such a lack of definitiveness in the English translations give us the *live option* of taking them all into account at once rather than fighting or stressing over which one is "right."

But let's look specifically at these verbs: *"become* a disciple," *instructed, trained.* The single Greek word behind all of these is μαθητευθεὶς | *mathēteutheis.* And so we look up the main verb form, μαθητεύω | *mathēteuō,* in a Greek lexicon.[18] There we see that the word is used in two general senses, and that several verbs phrases can be used in translation:

> (1) **intransitive** (has no direct object): implies being *an adherent of a teacher.* To be or become a pupil or disciple of someone; to be a follower; be taught or trained by a teacher; to adhere to a teacher. (Mt 13:52)

> (2) **transitive** (has a direct object): to make one a follower, a pupil or a disciple. To instruct, teach, train. (Mt 28:19)

Using a Greek lexicon is good because it will show you a summary of how a word *gets used* in some or all of its occurrences.[19] However, what is more fun (and often more revealing to you as a Bible reader) is to look up words yourself in some kind of concordance. So, using Bible software, you will find

---

[18] Like BDAG. A lexicon is a dictionary.

[19] Lexicons (dictionaries) of any kind or language (including English), do not show you the one and only *true meaning* of a word; they show you how words are/were *commonly used* in various contexts and locations. It is common that, over time, words change meaning.

(with only a couple of clicks) that μαθητεύω | *mathēteuō* occurs only 4 times (4x) in the entire Bible. [20] Namely: Mt 13:52; 27:57; 28:19; and Acts 14:21. This is suddenly very interesting. In Acts 14:21, the KJV has:

> And when they had preached the gospel to that city, and *had taught many* . . .

That is innocent enough. However, from the ASV onwards, translations have commonly said something like this:

> When they had preached the gospel to that city and had *made many disciples* . . . (RSV et al.)

Suddenly, now, we see that, in this context, this word is taken to imply more than merely teaching abstract or trivial things to people; the idea is rather that they instructed people to the point of becoming followers of Jesus.

All Matthew

Next we note that this word is a special term in Matthew, *not even occurring in any of the other Gospels.* This kind of "discovery" should jump off the page at us, like a flashing sign in the night. Looking closely at each of the three occurrences in Matthew (Mt 13:52; 27:57; 28:19), we look especially for how the word gets used, being careful not to impose meanings onto the word. For example, in 27:57, when Joseph of Arimathea shows up at crucifixion day's end, he is called "who also himself was discipled by Jesus." It is obvious that much more happened than "he was taught a few things" by Jesus. So also in 28:19, where the disciples are instructed to go and "make disciples," which implies people who become *adherents* to the person and teachings of Jesus. So we see that this word is not used merely to talk about teaching per se, but teaching to the point of decision to be a follower. This is a *powerful* word in context.

---

[20] "Entire Bible" means, here, the Greek Septuagint and New Testament. Remember, the Septuagint (often abbreviated LXX) is essentially the Greek OT and Apocrypha combined. For a fuller description see Collier 2018c, 22f.

We next might notice how Matthew also uses the noun form of this word, μαθητής | *mathētēs* (72x). Even this noun indicates more than a mere student. As one writer has put it:

> the emphasis in the common use of the term was not upon "learning," or upon being a "pupil," but upon adherence to a great master. Hence a "disciple" of Jesus . . . was one who adhered to his master, and the type of the adherence was determined by the master himself. [21]

It is clear, then, that the Gospel of Matthew is not talking about some trivial call — "come sell soap for me!" (It is not pop-religion.) Not at all. *The emphasis in Matthew is on what it means to be or become a disciple, a follower, an adherent of Jesus as Teacher, as Messiah, as Lord, as apocalyptic Son of Man, as proclaimer of the Kingdom of God!*

And so, when Jesus says in 13:52:

> . . . every scribe who has become *an adherent of me and my teachings* for the sake of the Kingdom of Heaven, that one is like a household manager who brings out from the storeroom things that are new and old,

he is at the very least showing a monumental difference between "taking a class" and "following a teacher."

Anticipation

There's more to this verse, and we will get to it. But just the small amount we have seen so far underscores that learning even a little Greek can help us become more *disciplined* students of the scriptures and begin to *open up a new world of understanding*. We start paying more attention to important detail; and we might even start hearing more of the voice of Jesus coming at us from behind the words we are reading.

If you are intimidated by the thought of learning Greek, it is time to turn that into *forward-looking anticipation*. Learning Greek is about becoming *disciplined readers* of our ancient texts; about being schooled for the Kingdom of Heaven. It is a *discipline*, and

---

[21] Wilkens 1988, 217.

if approached with care and a sense of expectation, it can be a *spiritual* discipline.

CONSIDER THE SPIRIT IN YOU

Before jumping into more Greek on the next page, it is very important that you **take up your journal and write** about the following questions:

1. What is the most important thing you have learned from this chapter about *being trained* for the Kingdom of Heaven?

2. Looking back at *Spiritual Benchmark #2*, in what ways do you anticipate that a study of NT Greek might open *a new world of understanding* for you?

3. Up to this point in this course, *just how much have you been praying that God might work on your heart to consider this as another possible avenue of the Spirit in your life?* However much, compose a prayer to that effect right now. Give it thought. Watch how writing this down causes you to think more deeply about what you are asking.

    (This question is asked like this so as to directly confront you with whether you are inviting the Spirit into this process, or deliberately keeping the Spirit out. Whatever your answer, don't hide from the question.)

    (Also, the point here is not at all that you are not really spiritual unless you study Greek. That would be absurd! The point is, rather, about whether you are inviting the Spirit of God to open your heart to such possibilities.)

TIME FOR GREEK: VERBS (2)

VOCABULARY

βασιλεία	"kingdom" (noun)
οὐρανός	"heaven, sky" (noun)
ἄνθρωπος	"a person, a human, a man" (noun)
αὐτός	"he" (pronoun) (αὐτοῦ ="of him"; αὐτοῖς ="to them"

MORE ON GREEK VERBS

Continuing from our previous lesson, let's look at verbs again, just to give you a little more time with them.

All the Verbs in Mt 13:52

εἶπεν: "he said" — A past tense form of λέγω, "I say."

μαθητευθεὶς: "having discipled" — A participle of μαθητεύω which means "I disciple, teach, train, etc." See previous lesson.

ἐστιν: "it is" — A present tense, 3rd singular of εἰμί, "I am." This is an extremely common word in Greek.

ἐκβάλλει: "he brings out" — A present tense of ἐκβαλλω. This is the easiest of all the forms on this list. Compare this with λύω chart on the previous page.

As stated, these are all the verbs in our focus text: Mt 13:52. At this point, there is no reason you should memorize what these forms are or how to recognize them. We will not focus on that kind of thing. (Besides, it would take too long to learn.) Allow this short list to illustrate that *verb forms may take many shapes.* That is the whole point here.

The Big Picture: The Greek Tense System

Just to give you an idea of the above principle (that *verb forms may take many shapes)*, what follows will be a chart that looks at the Greek verb system from 10,000 feet. This will show Greek *verb stems and flags that can go with them* (without all of the endings). Just like endings are *flags* that tell you how to translate, there are also other types of *flags* on Greek verbs. You know how this works in English: (I see, *will see*, *saw*, *have seen*). So in Greek, the verb stem adds different kinds of *flags* for what is needed in any given place:

*	Tense	Aug-ment		Dupli-cation		Stem		Tense Signifier		All Together	Endings**
Primary Tenses	Present					λυ	+	-	=	λυ-	ω,εις, etc.
	Future					λυ	+	σ	=	λυσ-	ω,εις, etc.
	Perfect			λε	+	λυ	+	κα	=	λελυκα-	-,ς,ε etc.
Second-ary Tenses	Imperfect	ε	+			λυ	+	-	=	ἐλυ-	ν,ς, -, etc.
	Aorist	ε	+			λυ	+	σα	=	ἐλυσα-	ν,ς, -, etc.
	Pluperfect	ε	+	λε	+	λυ	+	κει	=	ἐλελυκει-	ν,ς, -, etc.

*Naturally, the verb system is far more complicated. This chart is for illustration only.
**Endings shown are for illustration only; not all are technically accurate.

Table 4

Don't worry, you don't need to memorize this. The table simply gives you the "big picture" at a glance of the regular verb system (without all of the endings). This is merely to illustrate the point about *flags* on verbs.

TRANSLATE THIS

1. εἶπεν.

2. αὐτὸς εἶπεν.

3. ἄνθρωπος εἶπεν.

4. ἔστιν ἄνθρωπος.

5. αὐτός ἐστιν ἄνθρωπος.

6. οὐρανός ἐστιν βασιλεία.

7. μαθητεύω, μαθητεύει, μαθητεύετε.

8. κύριος μαθητεύει τοὺς γραμματεῖς καὶ ἐκβάλλουσιν
the   scribes

τὸν θησαυρόν.
the   treasure.

DISCIPLINE YOURSELF

This lesson has given you a bit more about Greek verbs. It is still highly simplified to help you take one step at a time.

1. Start with prayer about what it means for you *to be a disciple, a follower, an adherent of Jesus as Teacher, as Messiah, as Lord, as apocalyptic Son of Man, as proclaimer of the Kingdom of God!*

2. Review **the above Greek section** until you understand the principle it is trying to get across. Don't waste any time memorizing the tables. Write down any lingering questions.

3. Review all of your **vocabulary** every day. This is especially important since the vocab words will start to build up on you. You have now had 15 vocab words. Review them every day.

4. **Read Aloud:** As you have time, work on word pronunciation from the following text. Always pronounce the words aloud.

TRANSLATION KEY

(for the sentences on the previous page)

1. *"S/he said."*
2. *"He ~~(he)~~ said."* (αὐτός "he" is the subject.)
3. *"A man (person) ~~(he)~~ said."* (ἄνθρωπος is the subject.)
4. *"He is a man (person)."* (ἄνθρωπος is the predicate nominative.)
5. *"He is a man (person)."* (αὐτός "he" is the subject.)
6. *"Heaven is a kingdom."* (Heaven = subject; kingdom = pred nom.)
7. *"I disciple"; "s/he disciples"; "you (pl) disciple"* (Note the endings.)
8. *"The Lord ~~(he)~~ trains the scribes and they bring out the treasure."* ("Lord" is the subject; "~~(he)~~ trains" is 3rd sg; "they bring out" is 3rd pl.)

6
Kingdom of Heaven

SPIRITUAL BENCHMARK #3

The study of NT Greek can . . .
help you use English translations more profitably.

GUIDE TEXT:

ὁ δὲ εἶπεν αὐτοῖς· διὰ τοῦτο πᾶς γραμματεὺς μαθητευθεὶς
And he said to them: "Because of this, every scribe who has been trained

τῇ βασιλείᾳ τῶν οὐρανῶν ὅμοιός ἐστιν ἀνθρώπῳ οἰκοδεσπότῃ,
for **the Kingdom of Heaven**   **is like**   **a master** of a household,

ὅστις ἐκβάλλει ἐκ τοῦ θησαυροῦ αὐτοῦ καινὰ   καὶ   παλαιά.
who   brings out from   the treasure   of him new things and   old.

KINGDOM OF HEAVEN

How Many Times?

In all of the Bible, the phrase *Kingdom of Heaven* appears only in the Gospel of Matthew. It is always spoken by Jesus, and it occurs 32 times.

Or does it? Right off the bat, we run into an interesting problem in the existing English translations, because they don't all agree on how many times this phrase occurs. In fact, they vary: from 28x to 34x (that's a lot), and here is a small selection:[22]

28x = LEW
29x = ETH

---

[22] This is the result of a *BibleWorks* search in "Cross Version Search Mode," that took less than 15 seconds to set up and run. I have shown only a few of the translations. The full search reviewed about 40 translations. This attests to the great value of good Bible software for doing Bible study: nearly instant information.

31x = ERV, ASV
32x = KJV, RSV, NIV, and NET
33x = NJB, NLT, and CEB
34x = DRA

This kind of thing is why a few vocal Bible readers object to so many English translations: "They just confuse people!"

But this is a "stick your head in the sand" solution. In fact, there are actually quite good reasons for the differences, and they have to do with the Greek texts on which the translations are based. And all of that can get rather complicated. So then, even if you don't need or care to understand all of those reasons, *disciplined Bible readers* will care enough to value the fact that a variety of English translations show some difference on this and similar types of detail.

From this one technical point, we learn a principle for Bible study: **Multiple English translations can be a blessing. As conversation partners with us, they can alert English readers to issues and concerns that just one translation will not.** This can help us to be less dogmatic about our statements and more aware of the complications involved for any and every translation we might use.

Let's focus in, now, on how the phrase *Kingdom of Heaven* gets used in Matthew.[23]

What in the World is It?

Since Matthew uses *Kingdom of God* only 4 or 5 times,[24] it is fair to say that it *prefers* the former.[25]

You have likely heard Bible teachers remark (rightly) that both phrases are parallel and mean the same thing. (Obviously, both refer to a Kingdom not from this earth.) And you might also

---

[23] There is little doubt that 32x is the best number based on our available Greek texts. The complications of this go well beyond our purpose here.

[24] Mt 6:33; 12:28; 19:24; 21:31, 43, all spoken by Jesus.

[25] Other NT writings use *Kingdom of God* exclusively: Luke 31x + Acts 6 = 37x; Mark 14x; Paul 8x; John 2x.

have heard teachers say that Matthew's preference for *Kingdom of Heaven* is merely a reflection a Jewish tendency not to directly say the name of God — and maybe there is something to this. But then one starts to wonder why Matthew's Gospel uses the word *God* 44 times if it does not prefer using it. Perhaps it is not enough to say "the two phrases are identical." Maybe it is better to say this: Although both phrases clearly refer to God's Kingdom (clearly they do), Matthew's *Kingdom of Heaven*, within that Gospel, may be intending to shine a subtly different light.

Stay with me, here; this gets interesting. What I'm about to show cannot be seen from any English translation. In fact, many translations simply mask (hide, wash out) all of this. Also what I'm about to show can easily be overread, so one must be careful.

First let's deal in facts only. Heaven. The word is οὐρανός (which you now know and can pronounce) and is used in many texts to mean "heaven or sky."[26] Matthew uses this word:

27x as a singular noun
55x as a plural noun
32x in the phrase "Kingdom of Heaven." Every time, this phrase is plural: literally, "Kingdom *of the heavens*."

So what does it mean? Since the Gospel of Matthew

(1) is not shy about using the word *God*, and since it (2) always refers to the *Kingdom of Heaven* with the same phrase (βασιλεία τῶν οὐρανῶν), and (3) the word *heaven* is never singular in this phrase (like it is in many other Matthew texts), but always plural — then perhaps in Matthew this phrase is not only a circumlocution pointing to God himself (surely it points to God), but even more is *a reference to the realm of God in which he rules.* Matthew points to God, yes. But more: to *God, the ruler of the heavens!*[27] And this is seen especially in the next text.

---

[26] There is far more to this. BDAG lists three main points with many subpoints: (1) *heaven vs. earth* (mostly singular), e.g., where the stars are located; (2) *transcendent abode*, heaven, dwelling place of God; (3) *indirect reference to God.* Mostly, here, BDAG points to Matthew's "Kingdom of Heaven" for #3.

[27] I warn again against thinking that a mere or simplistic difference in singular or plural is at stake here, or that there is any sharp distinction between

As in Heaven

So let us pray for a moment. Matthew style. For early in the Gospel, Matthew's special interest[28] in *heaven* shows up: *The Lord's Prayer* (so-called). Since you already know the KJV version of this, I won't repeat it. But what I will do is retranslate it a little closer to the Greek text, keeping the words pretty much in order:

> Our Father, the one in the heavens:
>   May it be treated as holy — **your name!**[29]
>   May it arrive — **your pervasive rule [your Kingdom]**!
>   May it be accomplished — **your will!**
> as in heaven, so may it be on earth.
>
> The food we need each day,
>   may you grant us our portion for today;
> And may you forgive us our failings
>   as we have forgiven those who fail us;
> And may you carry us away from temptation
>   liberating us from the one who is evil.

Everyone can see that the prayer starts with *our Father in the heavens* and ends with *the evil one*. But not so obvious to all (get the KJV out of your head), immediately, three nouns *Name, Kingdom, Will* work together — all three — to point directly to *as in heaven, so on earth*. **The opening focus on God *in the heavens*, followed by *Name, Rule,* and *Will*, together build-up to the dénouement:** *The Rule [Kingdom] of Heaven on earth!*

Not so the beautifully poetic KJV: *Our Father who art in heaven, hallowed be thy name.* This actually turns the opening of the prayer into two couplets: *Father/Name* and *Kingdom/Will*. In the process, *as in heaven* is relegated to a mere tag-line for *Will*. This actually is a major shift, subverting the impact of this prayer in Matthew.

---

the Gospels; rather the emphasis is upon the dominant phrase *Kingdom of Heaven* as it gets used to govern Matthew's interest in what God is doing in the world.

[28] 82x in Mt, more than all others combined: 35x Lk; 18x Mk; 18x John.

[29] The version of this prayer most people know is certainly poetic and easy to remember. Unfortunately, it destroys the three-fold "Name; Rule; Will" parallelism and actually changes the focus of the prayer.

Luke does not have anything about *heaven* anywhere in its version of this prayer. It says quite simply:

Our Father
let it be sanctified — your name!
Let it come — your pervasive rule [your Kingdom]!
Give us our daily bread . . . etc.

Now the question is not, which one is right: Matthew or Luke? Each Gospel presents these as occurring at different times for different reasons. More importantly, our question should be: *What is each Gospel trying to tell us?*

Matthew has a special interest in heaven as the dwelling place of God, that place where God's name is kept holy, where his rule is already established, and where his will is done. And when we think about it, if this is how it is where God dwells, why would we not want it like that here where *we* dwell?

The Heart of It All

We move now to Matthew 13, to the heart of this Gospel. And here the phrase *Kingdom of Heaven* occurs nine times. No other Gospel does this. Matthew is doing something special.

So watch this: Out of the eight parables told,[30] *five of these are only in Matthew.* It is quite possible to see them all arranged by Matthew in a chiastic[31] formation (i.e., showing parallel relationships), like so:

---

[30] Commentators find either 7 or 8 parables. I agree with 8.

[31] I join other scholars in warning against uncontrolled applications of such structures as though they were secret codes concealing the "real hidden meanings" of authors. The internet is full of such exaggerations, and some individuals or groups focus on such structures one-sidedly, even seeing the Bible as one huge chiastic structure. This kind of overstatement is not useful. On the other hand, some scholars, having no ability to see such arrangements at all, like to throw the baby out with the bathwater, objecting with a myth of their own, that every item in a chiastic structure must be perfectly balanced at every point with another, or else it cannot exist. This is an erroneous view of the actual structures and functions of chiastic formulations, which might have a variety of functions: perhaps emphasis of meaning, or mere organization of material, or memory enhancement, or for balance in oral presentation, or more. See Vorster 1977; Wenham 1979; Collier 1993; contra Hagner 2000, 1:363, who dismisses the idea too easily for Matthew 13. Even so, I want to emphasize that my argument

A The Sower: **Those who hear** the word of the K/H (3-23)
  B The Weeds: The good and evil (24-30)
    C Mustard Seed and Leaven (Growth) (31-33)
    D Description of the K/H (34-43)
    C' Treasure and Pearl (Value) (44-46)
  B' The Net: The good and evil (vv. 47-50)
A' The Manager: **Those trained** for the K/H (51-52)

This is more than "a cool outline." We can notice that the bottom half is a kind of mirror image of the top, and that each item in the bottom is a kind of step up from the top. The center (D) describes or explains the Kingdom of Heaven,[32] and the outside edges (A/A') show reactions to the message, in which those trained have more responsibility than those who hear.

However, lest we get lost in fancy outlines (whether you think them real or imagined), my point is not dependent on such things. The role of the phrase *Kingdom of Heaven*, here, is unmistakable as a centerpiece for the Gospel. And what also cannot be missed, is that whether or not vv. 51-52 (our guide text) is considered a parable or not, this is the last occurrence of the phrase *Kingdom of Heaven* in the chapter (all the way until 16:19). *The focus of chapter 13 is entirely on the Kingdom of Heaven, and it comes to a culmination in 13:51-52.*

The final exuberant exhale of Jesus' teaching is 13:51-52, which follows the question, "Do you now (finally, at last) understand? When the answer is "Yes!" the next comment comes like a lightning bolt of responsibility: *Scribes trained for the Kingdom of Heaven know how to handle new and old!*

---

here is not dependent on the existence of any chiastic proposal. Instead, that structure would merely help underscore the point that Matthew 13 has been specially constructed to lead to Mt 13:51-52.

[32] Yes, it does much more than this: it is overtly the explanation of the parable of the weeds (found only in Matthew). However, in its current arrangement in Matthew, it occurs after the first four parables and before the last four, conveniently summarizing the Kingdom of Heaven for the disciples. That this arrangement is haphazard or accidental, or that it just happens to come after two other parables were told is hardly sensible. Just because an item may have multiple elements or functions does not prohibit it from having a larger function (as a whole) in the arrangement to which an author may be putting it.

This is no off-the-cuff or minor comment in the Gospel of Matthew, nor is it to be ignored as if it were veiled. This is a stark urging of preparation for the final commission in Mt 28:19ff.

CONSIDER THE SPIRIT IN YOU

Hopefully, the section above is helping to demonstrate the usefulness of Greek as a *spiritual* discipline. As a reminder, our goal together is not merely to learn Greek technicalities, or to replace English translations, but to consider how a knowledge of NT Greek can *help you use English translations more profitably.*

Now **take up your journal and write** about the following.

1. Write about the role of *heaven* in Matthew, how a closer look at the language helps to consider new spiritual possibilities.

2. Write about the "Lord's Prayer" in Matthew as it is laid out above. Since this is very hard to see in English texts, how could this help you pray this prayer in your life today?

3. Focus on the parable collection in Matthew 13 and on the role played there by the phrase *Kingdom of Heaven*. Write about how this might enlighten the meaning of Scribes trained for the Kingdom of Heaven in 13:51-52?

TIME FOR GREEK: NOUNS

VOCABULARY

οἰκοδεσπότης	"householder, manager of a house"
θησαυρός	"treasure, storehouse" (English *thesaurus*)
κύριος	"Lord, master"
θεός	"God"

NOUNS

Basics

General Notes: All Greek nouns have *gender, number,* and *case*.
   Gender = masculine (o()), feminine (h()), or neuter (to/).
   Number = singular or plural
   Case = five cases in all (here are the basic uses):

Nominative	(nom)	= subject
Genitive	(gen)	= possession
Dative	(dat)	= indirect object (i.o.)
Accusative	(acc)	= direct object (d.o.)
Vocative	(voc)	= direct address ("Son, arise!")
		(We will ignore the voc.)

Knowing the *case* of a Greek article or noun is extremely important. Only by knowing the *case* can you tell what is the subject of the verb and what is the direct object of the verb, etc. English and Greek have some similarities on this, but are enough different to warrant explanation.

(Note: The cases in English and Greek do not all have the same names, so the English cases will not be introduced here. For English cases, see standard English grammars.)

English

Look at this sentence and fill in the blanks below:
"The boy gave the bat of the coach to the fan."

FUNCTION	GREEK CASE
Subject: _____	(Nominative case)
Possession: _____	(Genitive case)
Indirect Object: _____	(Dative case)
Direct Object: _____	(Accusative case)

How did you know that *the boy* was the subject and that *the bat* was the direct object? Word order, right? So then, in English, the *order of the words* (i.e., *syntax*) in a sentence is what lets you know the subject from the direct object.

How did you know that the phrase *of the coach* showed possession and that the phrase *to the fan* was the indirect object? By the *flags* *of* and *to* with each word, right?

Now do this one:
"The coach gave the bat of the fan to the boy."

FUNCTION	GREEK CASE
Subject: _____	(Nominative case)
Possession: _____	(Genitive case)
Indirect Object: _____	(Dative case)
Direct Object: _____	(Accusative case)

In English, simply by changing a couple of words around, we can change the meaning of a sentence entirely. In fact, in English, for the words *man, boy,* and *coach* the form of the word does not tell you whether it is a subject or direct object. Word order does that.

Try another:

"The manager brings new things of his to the storeroom."

FUNCTION	GREEK CASE
Subject: _____	(Nominative case)
Possession: _____	(Genitive case)
Indirect Object: _____	(Dative case)
Direct Object: _____	(Accusative case)

Same dance, different tune. Not difficult.

Greek

Greek does not use word order in this way. Unlike English, Greek places a _flag_ on each noun to let you know whether it is a subject, or an object, or something else.

To illustrate, let's play a game. Suppose that

1. every English subject has -**_os_** at the end (e.g., boy**_os_**), and
2. every direct object has -**_on_** at the end (e.g., boy**_on_**).

Given those two rules, what would the following two sentences mean in English?

"The boy**_os_** hit the man**_on_** with the ball."

_____

"The boy**_on_** hit the man**_os_** with the ball."

_____

Flags

You can see that if English did this, it would not be _word order_ that determines the subject or object, but the _flags_ on the end of the words.[33]

---

[33] Obviously, _flags_ is not a technical term. It is just a word to help get the idea across. In 1st Year Greek, you learn the proper linguistic terms.

This is exactly what Greek does. The case is shown by *word form* (morphology) not *word order* (syntax). A *flag* on the end of a noun tells you what case it is and, so, what *function* it will have in the sentence.

Nouns have two basic parts: a *stem* and a *case ending*. The case endings will help you see *case, gender,* and *number* (singular or plural).

An example of one masculine noun, both singular and plural:

Sing-ular	Stem	+	Case End-ing	=	Noun	Translation
Nom	ἀνθρωπ-	+	-ος	=	ἄνθρωπος	"a person"
Gen	ἀνθρώπ-	+	-ου	=	ἀνθρώπου	"of a person"
Dat	ἀνθρώπ-	+	-ῳ	=	ἀνθρώπῳ	"to/for a person"
Acc	ἀνθρωπ-	+	-ον	=	ἄνθρωπον	"a person"
Plural						
Nom	ἀνθρωπ-	+	-οι	=	ἄνθρωποι	"people"
Gen	ἀνθρώπ-	+	-ων	=	ἀνθρωπῶν	"of people"
Dat	ἀνθρώπ-	+	-οις	=	ἀνθρώποις	"to/for people"
Acc	ἀνθρωπ-	+	-ους	=	ἀνθρώπους	"people"

Table 5

Ok, let's put this to use. Look at this next sentence.

ἄνθρωπ**ος** βλέπει ἀπόστολ**ον** = "A person sees an apostle"
a person   sees   an apostle

You know that ἄνθρωπ**ος** is the subject, not because of word order (even though it happens to be just like English, here), but because the end-*flag* (-**ος**) says, "I'm a nominative case."

However look at the next sentence carefully:

ἄνθρωπ**ον** βλέπει ἀπόστολ**ος** = _____
a person   sees   an apostle

How should this be translated? What is the subject? Object? If you wrote, "An apostle sees a person," you are correct.

For anyone who reads English, this example looks strange. The natural tendency of English speakers is to let the word order dictate what the subject is. But in this example, that would be incorrect. The subject is actually at the end of the sentence and the direct object is before the verb. (This is not unusual in Greek.) So, how do you know the subject from the object? By looking at the *case flags* at the end of the nouns.

The point of this entire exercise is very simple: **To read Greek nouns, you must know what case the noun is so that you can properly translate it. Hence, you must pay special attention to the case-endings of nouns.**

TRANSLATE THIS

1. κύριος εἶπεν λόγον ἀνθρώπῳ.

2. ἄνθρωπος εἶπεν λόγον κυρίῳ.

3. οἰκοδεσπότης μαθητεύει ἄνθρωπον.

4. ὁ δὲ εἶπεν αὐτοῖς λόγον κυρίου.

5. κύριος μαθητεύει ἄνθρωπον βασιλείᾳ αὐτοῦ.

DISCIPLINE YOURSELF

This lesson introduced Greek nouns. Naturally, everything we are doing in Greek is highly simplified, and you are not being given technical terminology.

This week:

1. Keep up with your **vocabulary** everyday!

2. Look over the Greek charts in this chapter until you understand how the noun is working. You do not need to memorize any of the charts.

3. Spend a little time looking at our *guide-text* at the beginning of the chapter. Reading the Greek out loud every day or two is still a very good idea. *Repetition is key.* It helps your brain get accustomed to the sight and sound of the language itself, but especially of the specific words of this sentence.

WARNING:

About now the excitement of learning to read the words of Jesus and the writers of the NT in the language they were written begins to fade for many first-time students. Alphabet, vocab words, verbs, nouns, charts, tables—all of it starts running together and things start getting a little blurry.

This is the trouble with any discipline: *it requires you to step up and do it.* Some advice:

1. Keep your focus on the spiritual reasons you came here.
2. Stay with the Greek material every day.

For this class it does not have to be a lot of time, but some every day is important. If you try to do this only one day a week, you are more likely to experience problems. Don't lie to yourself. That is not discipline.

I just gave you some very good advice. It is up to you to do it.

TRANSLATION KEY

(for the sentences two pages up)

1. *"(The) Lord said a word to a man."*
    κύριος in all examples here = "the Lord"
    κύριος is the subject of εἶπεν = The lord (he) said.
        Since κύριος is the subject, "he" is not needed.
        This cannot mean "'The Lord,' he said" or some such.
    λόγον is acc sg = direct object and tells *what* was said.
    ἀνθρώπῳ is dat sg = indirect object of the verb.

2. *"A man said a word to the Lord."*
    ἄνθρωπος nom sg = subject of εἶπεν = "a man (he) said."
    λόγον acc sg direct object of the verb
    κυρίῳ dat sg indirect object =to/for the Lord

3. *"A householder (he) trains a man."*
    οἰκοδεσπότης nom sg = subject of verb μαθητεύει
    ἄνθρωπον acc sg direct object

4. *"And he said to them a word of the Lord."*
    ὁ δὲ εἶπεν
        Simply treat this as a vocab word.
        δὲ = "and, but"; always second or later in its clause
        literally "and the one (he) said" = "and he said"
    αὐτοῖς dat plural = "to" or "for them"
    λόγον acc sg direct object
    κυρίου gen sg = "of the Lord" (shows whose word)

5. *"The Lord (he) trains a man for (the) kingdom of him."*
    κύριος nom sg subject of the verb
    μαθητεύει vb 3rd sg "he trains" = "The Lord (he) trains."
    ἄνθρωπον acc sg direct object
    βασιλείᾳ dat sg indirect object
    αὐτοῦ gen sg, showing possession. "Kingdom of him" = "his kingdom."
        The fact that it is his kingdom means it is definite = "the k/ of him."

7
Household Manager

SPIRITUAL BENCHMARK #4

*The study of NT Greek can . . .
take you beyond what English Bibles can provide.*

GUIDE TEXT:

ὁ δὲ εἶπεν αὐτοῖς· διὰ τοῦτο πᾶς γραμματεὺς μαθητευθεὶς
And he said to them: "Because of this, every scribe who has been trained

τῇ βασιλείᾳ τῶν οὐρανῶν ὅμοιός ἐστιν **ἀνθρώπῳ οἰκοδεσπότῃ**,
for the Kingdom of Heaven   is like   a master **of a household**,

ὅστις ἐκβάλλει ἐκ τοῦ θησαυροῦ αὐτοῦ καινὰ   καὶ   παλαιά.
who brings out from the treasure of him new things and   old.

HOUSEHOLD MANAGER

In all of the Bible, the word *householder* occurs only in the Synoptic Gospels. **Mark** has it only once at 14:13-14, where Jesus sends his disciples to town to ask a householder for a guestroom. **Luke** 22:11 is parallel to Mark (above), but Luke adds it three more times, all in stories told by Jesus: 12:39 (one who is ever watchful); 13:25 (one who locks a door); and 14:21 (one who gets angry when his invited guests turn him down).

Matthew

Matthew is a different story. Literally. Matthew omits this word in its parallel to Mark (above), saying only "go into town *to a certain one* and say . . ." (In itself, this is no big deal. But hold on, we are only getting started.) Matthew has stories similar to those just mentioned above in Luke, but they are each one in a different place in the overall Jesus story. For example, Mt 24:43 (cf. Lk 12:39) is virtually identical in wording, except in Matthew it is part of the "destruction of the temple" story and there is more emphasis placed on being alert. Mt 7:22 (cf. Lk 13:25) has "many people" instead of "householder." And Mt 14:21 (cf. Lk 14:21) has "king" instead of "householder," and the story turns quite violent. *All of this means that Matthew has only one occurrence of this word (24:43) in common with any other Gospel.*

We don't normally notice such things because we are too busy mashing the Gospels together into one big blob (to make sure they all say the same thing) instead of paying attention to some of the finer details. However, someone once said, *"the one who is faithful in little things is faithful in much"* (Lk 16:10). Sounds like good advice when dealing with biblical texts. Attention to detail can not only be character-building, it can be eye-opening.

So how does this help? Well, even the small amount of detail above suggests that Matthew may be using the word *householder* in a special way, different from Luke and especially from Mark. So to test this, let's keep going.

Looking closer we see that οἰκοδεσπότης | "householder" occurs in one form or another seven times (!) in Matthew alone. Now with this, we *really* get an indication that something special is going on in Matthew different from the others. And when we then discover that a sister word οἰκιακός | "household member, family member" occurs two times, and only in Matthew, we begin to see that we have struck some kind of treasure.

What we do, then, is simply look up each text in Matthew and ask, *How is this functioning here?*

10:25	Jesus is *householder*; the disciples are *family members*
13:27	The apocalyptic Son of Man is *householder*
13:52	[This is our verse we are trying to test.]
20:1	Jesus as judge is the *householder*
20:11	Jesus as judge is the *householder*
21:33	God is *householder*, with Jesus as son/stone.
24:43	Each disciples is the *householder,* watching and alert.

When we next look at the sister-word, οἰκιακός | "family member" (10:25, 36) and see that they both point directly to the disciples, we come to see that *from the very first use of "household master and member"* in this Gospel, these words point directly to Jesus and disciples.

Two times, then, the word οἰκοδεσπότης | "householder" refers to the disciples themselves (13:52 and 24:43), and it becomes clear in 13:52 that by watching the Teacher handle what is old and what is new up to this point, each disciple, now, as the householder (the scribe trained for the Kingdom of heaven), knows how to handle such treasure.

Household Work

What does this have to do with Greek? Could we not have done this same thing knowing only English? *The fact is,* there are ways of going over the river and through the woods using Young's or Strong's concordance to do something similar, not knowing any Greek. Furthermore, the star-lit promise of some Bible software salespeople is that "you now don't need to know any Greek to perform such studies!" (Just remember, these are salespeople.) However, *the rest of this story is* that doing even a brief word study without any Greek background, even with the best Bible software in the world, can leave you making subtle mistakes and drawing incorrect conclusions.

Bible software is great! As long as you don't buy the line that "you don't have to know anything to do a real Greek study!" Using Bible software in that fashion is nothing more than opening another commentary, where somebody else tells you what to think. The best use of such software is when you know what you are doing and then you use the software to help you do your own work. Knowing something about Greek is vital for that and can *take you beyond what English Bibles and English study aids can provide.*

Tools and Such

So look at how we have proceeded so far. We did not run to a commentary or even a dictionary to start. Rather, we used Bible software to look up the Greek text, and then we did a word search on specific words. Because our word was οἰκοδεσπότης ("householder") we immediately looked it up concordance-style to see its uses for ourselves. Why? Because we don't want anyone else telling us what to think about the word we are looking up; we want to see it in action in actual texts for ourselves first. Then, after that, we certainly want to see what others have to say.

To illustrate, had we gone first to the best Greek dictionary available (BDAG), we would have seen this entry:

οἰκοδεσπότης, ου, ὁ (οἶκος, δεσπότης; later word [Lob., Phryn. p. 373]; Alexis Com. [IV BC] 225; Plut., Mor. 271e; SIG 888, 57f; New Docs 2, 58 no. 18,12 [75/76 AD]; Isaurian ins in PASA III p. 150 υἱοὺς τοὺς οἰκοδεσπότας; PLond I, 98 recto, 60 p. 130 [I/II AD]; PSI 158, 80 (for astrol. pap [incl. PParis 19, 42; 75, 10f; PLond I, 110, 41 p. 132 [138 AD]] s. Neugebauer-Hoesen index); TestJob 39:2; Philo; Jos., C. Ap. 2, 128) *master of the house, householder* Mt 24:43; Mk 14:14; Lk 12:39. Pleonast. οἰκ. τῆς οἰκίας Lk 22:11 (cp. SIG 985, 52 [II/I BC]; s. B-D-F §484). Used w. ἄνθρωπος in a figure Mt 13:52; 20:1; 21:33. In parables and figures, of God (cp. Epict. 3, 22, 4; Philo, Somn. 1, 149) 13:27 (interpreted as the Human One in vs. 37); 20:1, 11; 21:33; Lk 14:21; Hs 5, 2, 9; cp. IEph 6:1. Christ of himself Mt 10:25; Lk 13:25 (δεσπότης P[75]). — DELG s.v. δεσπότη. M-M. TW.

BDAG is a very important resource. However, had we started here, we might not have done a concordance search at all, thinking we already know *what the word means*. How could we top BDAG? If you look at that entry above, it is quite technical. However, it does not at all make clear *how that meaning might be functioning* in Matthew. (In other words, just because it means *householder* in all texts does not tell us how the word is being applied.) And it does not point out οἰκιακός ("family member") at all. The only way to see such things is to do your own work based on a Greek text, which means starting with a concordance investigation — like rummaging through a room full of treasures. This way, before listening to what anyone else says, you become personally familiar with the text for yourself.

To Infinity and Beyond

Pursuing a lifetime study of NT Greek as a spiritual discipline does not mean that you must become a "Greek scholar." If you become one, great! But that does not need to be your goal. Just staying with this language as you study the Bible can not only help you understand your English Bibles and English study aids (including Bible software), it can take you beyond.

CONSIDER THE SPIRIT IN YOU

Doing household chores (making the bed, washing dishes or clothes, dusting, sweeping) these do not sound too spiritual. But how wonderful it feels to sit down in a clean home with chores done!

Then there is this text:

> Whatever you find to do with your hands, do it with all your might, because there is neither work nor planning nor knowledge nor wisdom in the grave, the place where you will eventually go. (NET Eccl. 9:10; cf 1Sam 10:7)

James adds to this:

> What is your life? You are a vapor that shows up for a short time only to dissipate. (Jas 4:14)

And finally, a more popular aphorism, and not as powerful, says this: "Make hay while the sun shines."

Spiritual quests attempt to make sense out of the short lives we all have. That is why approaching the tasks of learning Greek are like the work of a household manager. Understood and approached properly, they can make ultimate spiritual sense.

Now **take up your journal and write**:

1. What impresses you the most about *householder* from the Gospel of Matthew?

2. How would you compare, contrast, or relate the study of NT Greek to being a household manager?

TIME FOR GREEK: "THE"

VOCABULARY

εἰμι	"I am"
ἐγώ	"I" (emphatic form pronoun)
διὰ τοῦτο	"because of this" (preposition + adj)
εὐαγγέλιον, -ου, τό	"the gospel, the good news"
ὁ, ἡ, τό	"the"

24 WAYS TO SAY "THE"

Basics

Greek has no indefinite article ("a" or "an").

The Greek definite article ("the"), like nouns, has *gender, number,* and *case.*

Gender	= masculine (ὁ), feminine (ἡ), or neuter (τό)
Number	= singular or plural
Case	= five cases in all (following are the basic uses):

Nominative	= subject of a verb
Genitive	= possession, relationship
Dative	= indirect object
Accusative	= direct object
Vocative	= direct address (as in "Son, come here")
	(We will ignore this case.)

As noted in the previous chapter, knowing the *case* of a Greek article or noun is extremely important. Only by knowing the *case* can you tell what is the subject of the verb and what is the direct object of the verb, etc.

Forms

One of the easiest ways to recognize the case of a noun is by looking at its definite article: *they will always agree in case, gender, and number.* Here are the 24 forms of the Greek definite article:

	Singular			Plural			
	M	F	N	M	F	N	
Nom	ὁ	ἡ	τό	οἱ	αἱ	τά	"the"
Gen	τοῦ	τῆς	τοῦ	τῶν	τῶν	τῶν	"of the"
Dat	τῷ	τῇ	τῷ	τοῖς	ταῖς	τοῖς	"to / for the"
Acc	τόν	τήν	τό	τούς	τάς	τά	"the"

Table 6

Memorize this chart like so: *singular* first, across for each case (ὁ, ἡ, τό), then (τοῦ, τῆς , τοῦ), and so on. Then *plural*.

General Rule

Translate the definite article when it occurs, but not when it doesn't. This does not always work, but it is the right place to start. Since there is no indefinite article ("a, an") in Greek, when a noun appears without a definite article, the noun is usually indefinite.

> Example: ὁ λόγος = "the word"
> λόγος = "a word" or just "word"

All such "rules" have exceptions which must be learned through time and experience. For example, the article is often used with personal names (e.g., ὁ Ἰησοῦς) but is not translated. In all instances, context is needed to make a decision.

Declensions/Patterns

There are three major pattern-groups (called declensions) by which nouns are formed. We are not going to learn those, but here is a greatly oversimplified example of three masculine nouns:

1st Declension	2nd Declension	3rd Declension
ὁ μαθητής	ὁ λόγος	ὁ γραμματεύς

Important: Nouns may vary by declension; the article does not.

Lexicons

Lexicons list each noun with its article and genitive case. The Genitive case shows what declension the noun belongs to. Even though we are not learning the declensions, you should always learn vocabulary nouns as listed below.

noun + genitive ending + article. Like so:

λόγος, -ου, ὁ	"the word"
οὐρανός, -ου, ὁ	"the heaven"
ἄνθρωπος, -ου, ὁ	"the man, the person"
οἰκοδεσπότης, -ου, ὁ	"the household manager"
θησαυρός, -ου, ὁ	"the treasure"
κύριος, -ου, ὁ	"the Lord"
θεός, -ου, ὁ	"the God"
γραμματεύς, έως, ὁ	"the scribe"
βασιλεία -ας, ἡ	"the kingdom
εὐαγγέλιον, -ου, τό	"the gospel, the good news"

Examples

Look over the sentences on the next page from Matthew to see how the article looks with nouns in actual texts. *You will hopefully recognize a few things, but you are not expected to be able to translate these. Just look for the marked articles and have fun with the rest.*

You should not need to spend very long on this.

Also, note that these are the seven *householder* texts in Matthew.

1. ἀρκετὸν **τῷ** μαθητῇ ἵνα γένηται ὡς

   It is enough **for the** disciple   to be   like

   ὁ διδάσκαλος αὐτοῦ καὶ **ὁ** δοῦλος ὡς **ὁ** κύριος αὐτοῦ.

   the teacher   of him   and **the** slave   like **the** lord   of him

   εἰ **τὸν** οἰκοδεσπότην Βεελζεβοὺλ ἐπεκάλεσαν,

   If   **the**   householder   "Beelzebul"   they called

   πόσῳ μᾶλλον **τοὺς** οἰκιακοὺς αὐτοῦ.

   how much more   **the**   household members   of him?   (Mt 10:25)

   Notes for above:

τῷ μαθητῇ*	**for the** disciple	dat	masc	sg
ὁ διδάσκαλος	**the** teacher	nom	masc	sg
ὁ δοῦλος	**the** slave	nom	masc	sg
ὁ κύριος	**the** lord	nom	masc	sg
τὸν οἰκοδεσπότην*	**the** householder	acc	masc	sg
τοὺς οἰκιακοὺς	**the** household members	acc	masc	pl

   *Articles **always** agree in case, gender, number (cgn), **even if they don't look the same as the noun ending.** The article tells you the cgn. Now notice that "they" is the subject and "householder" is the direct object — here it is moved forward in the sentence for emphasis.* You won't see this from an English text.

2. προσελθόντες δὲ **οἱ** δοῦλοι **τοῦ** οἰκοδεσπότου

   having come   **the** slaves   **of the** householder

   εἶπον αὐτῷ· κύριε, οὐχὶ καλὸν σπέρμα ἔσπειρας

   said   to him   "Lord,   not   good   seed   you sowed

   ἐν **τῷ** σῷ ἀγρῷ;

   in   the   your   field?   (Mt 13:27)

3. πᾶς γραμματεὺς μαθητευθεὶς

   every   scribe   who has been trained

   τῇ βασιλείᾳ **τῶν** οὐρανῶν

   for the Kingdom   **of the** heavens

   ὅμοιός ἐστιν ἀνθρώπῳ οἰκοδεσπότῃ,

   is like   **a** man   **a** householder,

ὅστις ἐκβάλλει ἐκ   τοῦ θησαυροῦ αὐτοῦ
who   brings out   from   **the**   treasure   of him. (Mt 13:52)

4. Ὁμοία γάρ ἐστιν **ἡ** βασιλεία **τῶν** οὐρανῶν
    like   for   it is   **the** Kingdom   **of the** heavens

    ἀνθρώπῳ οἰκοδεσπότῃ, ὅστις ἐξῆλθεν ἅμα πρωΐ
    a man   a householder,   who   went out   early in the morning

    μισθώσασθαι ἐργάτας εἰς **τὸν** ἀμπελῶνα αὐτοῦ.
    to hire   workers   for **the**   vineyard   of him. (Mt 20:1)

5. λαβόντες δὲ ἐγόγγυζον κατὰ **τοῦ** οἰκοδεσπότου
    having received [pay]   they grumbled   against   **the**   householder. (Mt 20:11)

6. ἄνθρωπος ἦν   οἰκοδεσπότης ὅστις ἐφύτευσεν
    a man   there was   **a** householder   who   planted

    ἀμπελῶνα.
    a vineyard (Mt 21:33)

7. εἰ ᾔδει   **ὁ** οἰκοδεσπότης   ποίᾳ φυλακῇ
    if   had known **the** householder   what   watch [time]

    ὁ κλέπτης ἔρχεται, . . . οὐκ ἂν εἴασεν διορυχθῆναι
    the thief   was coming . . .   he would not have allowed to be broken into

    τὴν οἰκίαν αὐτοῦ.
    the   house   of him.   (Mt 24:43)

As mentioned above, all definite articles and nouns have case, gender, and number. When articles are used with nouns, they will **agree in all three** (CGN).

TRANSLATE THIS

Don't let this scare you. You've been learning vocab and we have been using all of these things in our examples up to now.

1. ὁ οἰκοδεσπότης μαθητεύει τὸν ἄνθρωπον τῇ βασιλείᾳ

   τῶν οὐρανῶν.

2. διὰ τοῦτο, ὁ θεὸς ἐκβάλλει τοὺς ἀνθρώπους

   ἐκ τῆς βασιλείας αὐτοῦ

   καὶ μαθητεύει τὸν οἰκοδεσπότην.

DISCIPLINE YOURSELF

This lesson introduced the Greek definite article.

1. Start with a **prayer of thanksgiving** that you are being allowed to look at some of the details of the language of the New Testament.

2. Memorize the definite **article chart**. (See the practice charts two pages down.)

3. Naturally, keep up with your **vocabulary** everyday. (If you don't do that now, it will slip away.)

TRANSLATION KEY

(for the sentences on the previous page)

1. *"The householder trains the man for the Kingdom of Heaven."*

    ὁ οἰκοδεσπότης nom masc sg (note the article) subject of the verb
    μαθητεύει 3rd sg "s/he trains"= "The householder ~~(he)~~ trains."
    τὸν ἄνθρωπον acc sg masc direct object
    τῇ βασιλείᾳ dat sg fem indirect object = "to" or "for the kingdom"
    τῶν οὐρανῶν gen pl literally "of the heavens."
    An idiom for "of heaven"

2. *"Because of this, God brings out the men (people) from the kingdom of him (his kingdom) and he trains the householder."*

    διὰ τοῦτο Treat this as a vocab word: "because of this".
    διὰ is a preposition; "because of" or "on account of" with acc.
    τοῦτο acc sg "this"
    ὁ θεὸς lit "the God", but translate simply "God"
    nom subject of the verb ἐκβάλλει = "God ~~(he)~~ brings out."
    ἐκβάλλει 3rd sg, "he brings out" or "he throws out" (either works)
    The context will have to tell you which is more likely.
    τοὺς ἀνθρώπους acc pl direct object = "the men"
    (Notice agreement of article and noun.)
    ἐκ τῆς βασιλείας αὐτοῦ "from the kingdom of him"
    This is a prepositional phrase.
    ἐκ a preposition that takes gen case = "out of" or "from"
    τῆς βασιλείας gen sg "of the kingdom" (notice the article)
    αὐτοῦ gen case "of him" or "his"; shows relationship
    καὶ "and"
    μαθητεύει 3rd sg "he trains"
    τὸν οἰκοδεσπότην acc sg masc direct object of the verb telling who is
    getting trained.

    Notice that you have one subject and two verbs:
    ὁ θεὸς   ἐκβάλλει . . . καὶ μαθητεύει . . .

LEARN THE ARTICLE BY HEART

(Make copies, and practice)

	Singular			Plural		
	M	F	N	M	F	N
N						
G						
D						
A						

	Singular			Plural		
	M	F	N	M	F	N
N						
G						
D						
A						

	Singular			Plural		
	M	F	N	M	F	N
N						
G						
D						
A						

(Make copies, and practice)

	Singular			Plural		
	M	F	N	M	F	N
N						
G						
D						
A						

	Singular			Plural		
	M	F	N	M	F	N
N						
G						
D						
A						

	Singular			Plural		
	M	F	N	M	F	N
N						
G						
D						
A						

8
Treasure

SPIRITUAL BENCHMARK #5

The study of NT Greek can . . .
make you less dependent on others for reading the Bible.

GUIDE TEXT:

ὁ δὲ εἶπεν αὐτοῖς· διὰ τοῦτο πᾶς γραμματεὺς μαθητευθεὶς
And he said to them: "Because of this, every scribe who has been trained

τῇ βασιλείᾳ τῶν οὐρανῶν ὅμοιός ἐστιν ἀνθρώπῳ οἰκοδεσπότῃ,
for the Kingdom of Heaven   is like   a master of a household,

ὅστις ἐκβάλλει ἐκ τοῦ θησαυροῦ αὐτοῦ καινὰ   καὶ   παλαιά.
who   brings out **from   the treasure** **of him** new things and   old.

TREASURE

One of my favorite childhood books was *Treasure Island*, by Robert Louis Stephenson: pirates, maps, X marks the spot! This is more than entertaining; it is a mesmerizing, enthralling adventure!

Matthew

Treasure is the word used by Jesus in Matthew to describe spiritual teachings and texts. And just like *householder*, so now *treasure* is used once in Mark (10:21), four times in Luke (6:45; 12:33, 34; 18:22) and nine times in Matthew (see below). This Gospel is at it again:

2:11	Wise men bring treasures to child Jesus in a house.
6:19, 20, 21	Treasures on earth vs. heaven; treasure and heart.
12:35	Good *brings out* good treasure. Evil *brings* evil.
13:44	K/H is a hidden treasure worth everything!
13:52	*He brings out* new and old things.
19:21	Treasure in heaven is not money.

This is not some duplicate of Mark and Luke. Nor is it merely "additional historical tidbits" to be added to those other Gospels to manufacture a "real life of Jesus." This is Matthew shaping and developing his story. Here Jesus, his actions, his teachings, and his message of the Kingdom of Heaven are altogether a treasure too often hidden and forgotten but worth all that one can ever have or do or believe. This treasure holds secrets, new and old, and the one trained in such things knows how to bring them out.

Bringing Out

What jumps off the page to anyone reading a Greek text is the similarity of two of the above texts: 12:35 and 13:52.

12:35: ὁ ἀγαθὸς ἄνθρωπος ἐκ τοῦ ἀγαθοῦ θησαυροῦ *ἐκβάλλει* ἀγαθά, καὶ ὁ πονηρὸς ἄνθρωπος ἐκ τοῦ πονηροῦ θησαυροῦ *ἐκβάλλει* πονηρά.

The good person from the good treasure *brings out* good things; and the evil person from the evil treasure *brings out* evil things.

It is not simply this word ("brings out") that is of interest, but how this word occurs in two such similar contexts in Matthew's own Gospel—as if one enlightens the other:

13:52: πᾶς γραμματεὺς μαθητευθεὶς τῇ βασιλείᾳ τῶν οὐρανῶν ὅμοιός ἐστιν ἀνθρώπῳ οἰκοδεσπότῃ, ὅστις *ἐκβάλλει* ἐκ τοῦ θησαυροῦ αὐτοῦ καινὰ καὶ παλαιά.

Every scribe trained for the Kingdom of Heaven is like a householder who *brings out* of his treasure new things and old.

Clearly, in Matthew, the one trained to know how to *bring out* such things is trained in what is good—to know the difference between the good and evil paths. That one is trained to handle new and old teachings, and the sacred writings themselves: how they point to Jesus as Christ; how they are corrupted by the teachings of the Pharisees. In this Gospel, there is a difference in the path of Jesus and that of the Pharisees. Jesus' followers are trained to know the difference and to follow suit.

Models

We even have an example of this—an actual scribe trained for the Kingdom of Heaven—bringing out new things and old from the sacred scriptures.

We can see it right in Matthew, over and over again: Matthew is concerned to show Jesus as the new Moses; and Jesus' teachings are both the new Torah and the correct way of reading the Torah. Sixteen times Matthew uses the verb πληρόω ("to fulfil") to show how to *bring out* from what is old (the sacred texts) something new: that Jesus is the promised Christ! Of course, there is much, much more in Matthew. Some have even suggested that Matthew himself is the scribe trained for the Kingdom of Heaven and that there is a play on the two words: Μαθθαῖος ("Matthew") and μαθητεύω ("to train"). But whether that was intended or not, the Gospel of Matthew clearly charges the disciples of Jesus with knowing how to bring both new and old things from the Jesus-treasures.

In addition to Matthew, another clear example is Paul in numerous texts.[34] Let's take just one:

2 Cor 4:5-7: [5]Oh yes! It is Jesus Christ as KURIOS that we proclaim, not ourselves! We are merely your slaves for the sake of Jesus. [6]After all, the God who said *"Let light shine out of darkness,"* he is the one who shined in our hearts to enlighten us fully, namely that in the very face of Christ, that is how we come to know God's glory!

[7]But in jars of baked clay we have this *treasure*;
it is God's and not ours, this power beyond measure![35]

This is an astonishing example! Paul is either quoting a text we no longer have—*"Let light shine out of darkness"*—or he is summarizing or repeating an idea found in scattered texts (Gen 1:3; Ps 112:4; Job 37:15; Isa 9:1). Whatever the case, he is caught in the very act, here, of *bringing out* things both new and old. We

---

[34] Among the best examples, cf. Rom 10:5-23; 1Cor 10:1-13; Eph 4:8-10.

[35] For more on this text see Collier 2012, 124ff.

must not miss this. He is bringing to a culmination his interpretive conversation with Exodus 34, *explaining, bringing out* about Moses and the veil only a few verses above. In fact, says Paul, *the glory of God is not known in Moses, whose glory was fading, but in the face of Christ – that is where we see the unfading glory of God!*

This he now calls a *treasure!* And it happens by the power of God, not by anything he (or we) can say or do.

Matthew and Paul are both making Christ known to their readers. As disciplined readers, we respect their individual contexts and efforts as written documents. We do not just mash them together. However, we must not make the mistake of thinking that we are now outsiders to these kinds of conversations presented by Matthew and Paul—conversations where the treasure awaits. Indeed, we are called to participate in them. Because in Χριστός, X truly does mark the spot.

CONSIDER THE SPIRIT IN YOU

Being dependent on others is a fact of life for many things. *We need each other – and certainly we need the Holy Spirit of God!* At the same time, we know that too much dependency on other people can stunt both our growth and the Spirit of God in us.

One of the big promises that a study of NT Greek makes is a more direct access to the texts of the Bible. There is something wonderfully *liberating and exhilarating* about looking directly at the actual words of biblical texts instead of through the dark glass of somebody else's translation of it. It is a treasure, indeed, when we are better able to evaluate the ancient words that are right in front of us. We will always need each other—that will never change. But we will be *less dependent* on what others tell us the words in biblical texts mean.

After some careful thought, **take up your journal and write**:

1. What did you learn about the phrase *"bringing out"* from this chapter?

2. Consider, as a *disciplined* reader of the Bible, the following question:

    How does the treasure spoken of by Jesus in Mt 13:52 inform how you see yourself as a disciple and how you approach reading the Bible?

3. Knowing that Jesus is not saying *"If you will be my disciple, you will learn Greek!"* in Mt 13:52, is it possible for you to see (by metaphorical extension) your study of Greek as a part of the *treasure* talked about by Jesus? If so, write about that. If not, what is stopping you from seeing it?

TIME FOR GREEK: ADJECTIVES (1)

VOCABULARY

καινός, -ή, -όν	"new"
καλός, -ή, -όν	"good, beautiful"
νεός, -ά, -όν	"new" (*neo*natal)
ὅμοιος, οία, ον	"like"
παλαιός -ά, -όν	"old"

ADJECTIVES

This will be an extremely simplified look at adjectives.

In English, an adjective modifies a noun or adjective. Like this:

1. The **red** dog on the **blue** tree.
2. Do you like my **ever-lovin'** hat, for cry'n out loud?
3. (from some **poor** guy who has read this **charming** story one too many times)

In Greek, sentence #1 might look like either one of these:
Either: The **red** dog
Or: The dog the **red** (= the red dog)

They both mean the same thing.

The Case, Gender, Number Rule:
Because adjectives modify nouns, they have masculine, feminine, and neuter forms, just like the definite article does. (Reviewing the article chart in lesson 7 might be useful here. The better you know that chart, the easier adjective forms are.)

Articles, nouns, and adjectives all have case, gender, and number.
If they modify each other, they all must agree.

One Lick of a Lollipop

Here comes a mere taste of something extremely important:

Ἐγώ εἰμι ὁ καλὸς ποιμήν.
I   am   the   good   shepherd.

In this sentence, the adjective is in the **attributive position**: i.e., the adjective attributes some quality directly to the noun.

Because this is exactly like English, this is easy both to see and understand. However, there is much more to the Greek adjective that is very different from English, and we *are going to skip all of it*. Some of it is not quite so easy, and it is all crucial for translating Greek word order (syntax), even to the level of advanced sentences.

We are leaving all of that extra detail out. This is a pre-grammar, not a grammar. So here, you are only getting a very small taste of it, like one lick of a lollipop. [36]

Now, coming back to our sentence, look again:

Ἐγώ εἰμι ὁ [**καλὸς**] ποιμήν.
I   am   the   good   shepherd.

Just like English, the article *the* actually goes with the noun *shepherd*. This is not just any shepherd; this is the *good* shepherd. Notice that all of these are in the same case, gender, and number.

Now let's take a very small look at what adjectives might look like on the next page.

---

[36] Ok, here's another lick. Actually, Jn 10:11 is written like this:
Ἐγώ εἰμι ὁ ποιμὴν ὁ **καλός** = "I am the shepherd, the good [one]." But it is translated "I am the good shepherd." English does not do anything like this, so it is more challenging for new students. Greek will use both methods. Although in some contexts, this way of placing the adjective at the end may be slightly more emphatic, this is debated and is better learned as two ways of saying the same thing.

What Adjectives Look Like

Since adjectives agree in *case, gender, and number* with their articles and nouns, they can be any gender: masculine, feminine, or neuter. So they have numerous forms:

Singular

	M.	F.	N.
N.	καινός	καινή	καινόν
G.	καινοῦ	καινῆς	καινοῦ
D.	καινῷ	καινῇ	καινῷ
A.	καινόν	καινήν	καινόν
V.	καινέ	καινή	καινόν

Plural

	M.	F.	N.
N.V.	καινοί	καιναί	καινά
G.	καινῶν	καινῶν	καινῶν
D.	καινοῖς	καιναῖς	καινοῖς
A.	καινούς	καινάς	καινά

Table 7

This is just one pattern, so be aware that there are other patterns that we are not going to cover. For example, for the word παλαιός, -ά, -όν, the feminine singulars have the following endings: -ά, - ᾶς, -ᾷ, -άν, instead of the η. The main thing for now is that you get the idea that adjectives have case, gender, and number forms (to match whatever nouns they are used with).

Looking-Up Adjectives:

Adjectives are shown in lexicons as follows so as to indicate the case, gender, and number pattern:

καινός, -ή, -όν   "new"
παλαιός, -ά, -όν   "old"

TRANSLATE THIS

To understand the following, make sure you look carefully at the case, gender, and number of the adjectives.

1. ὁ καινὸς ἄνθρωπος ἐκβάλλει τὸν καίνον λόγον τοῦ

   εὐαγγελίου ἐκ* τοῦ καινοῦ θησαυροῦ.

   *ἐκ is a preposition that is always followed by a genitive case word or phrase. So, ἐκ τοῦ καινοῦ θησαυροῦ (all genitive case) is a *prepositional phrase*. Translate ἐκ τοῦ as either *"out of the"* or *"from the."*

2. ὁ παλαιὸς ἄνθρωπος ἐκβάλλει τὸν παλαιὸν λόγον

   τῆς βασιλείας ἐκ* τοῦ παλαιὸυ γραμματέως.**

   *ἐκ = same as above. Here the phrase is ἐκ τοῦ παλαιὸυ γραμματέως.

   **What case is this noun? Hint: look at the article, even though it is two words earlier (article + adjective + noun, as two pages earlier). The article will always tell you the case, gender, and number of its noun and/or adjective.

DISCIPLINE YOURSELF

1. **Translate** the sentences above.
2. Keep up with your **vocabulary** everyday.
3. Read the Greek section of the chapter as much as needed to get the principles being taught. You do **not** need to memorize the **adjective chart.**
4. Keep reviewing and practicing the **definite article chart.** You should be able to say it and write it.

TRANSLATION KEY

(for the sentences two pages up)

1. *"The new man brings out the new word of the Gospel from the new treasure."*
   Note how "the new man" is nominative subject, and "the new word" is accusative direct object.

   ὁ καινὸς ἄνθρωπος Nom art + adj + noun: all agree in cgn. The subject.

   ἐκβάλλει Verb, 3ʳᵈ sg "he brings out"; "he" is not needed in translation because of the subject ὁ καινὸς ἄνθρωπος. Hence, "the new man ~~(he)~~ brings out."

   τὸν καίνον λόγον Acc art + adj + noun: all agree in cgn. Direct object.

   τοῦ εὐαγγελίου Gen art + adj + noun: shows some kind of relationship. For now it is enough to translate "*of* the Gospel." The need to interpret what "*of*" means here is something for more advanced translation.

   ἐκ τοῦ καινοῦ θησαυροῦ. Preposition + art + adj + noun. As described above, ἐκ takes the gen case, so we have a prepositional phrase in the genitive case, *"of the new treasure."*

2. *"The old man brings out the old word of the kingdom from the old scribe."*
   Note how "the old man" is nominative subject, and "the old word" is accusative direct object.

   The grammatical notes are virtually the same as the previous example.

9
New

The study of NT Greek can . . .
broaden your spiritual vocabulary.

GUIDE TEXT:

ὁ δὲ εἶπεν αὐτοῖς· διὰ τοῦτο πᾶς γραμματεὺς μαθητευθεὶς
And he said to them: "Because of this, every scribe who has been trained

τῇ βασιλείᾳ τῶν οὐρανῶν ὅμοιός ἐστιν ἀνθρώπῳ οἰκοδεσπότῃ,
for the Kingdom of Heaven   is like   a master of a household,

ὅστις ἐκβάλλει ἐκ τοῦ θησαυροῦ αὐτοῦ **καινὰ**   καὶ   παλαιά.
who   brings out   from   his treasure   **new things**   and   old.

NEW

"New" can be exciting! It can open doors, provide solutions, bring refreshment, reinvigorate a lagging spirit, and mend a broken heart. For any human being or organization, there is nothing quite like "a breath of fresh air" or "new blood" to bring new life and a sense of meaning.

Learning Greek

Learning NT Greek can take on just that kind of role in one's Bible study life. Instead of continually telling yourself how intimidating, or scary, or difficult it is, one could simply ask,

*How many Bible study doors will a study of this language open for me if I simply approach it as a **spiritual** tool?*

*How much more insight and understanding will I gain when reading the Bible if I approach NT Greek as a **spiritual** discipline?*

How much better will I understand my English translations of the New Testament if I realize that all such translation is an effort to make plain in English what the Greek text was attempting to convey?

How much could my spiritual vocabulary be broadened by working not only in English, but in the language in which the text was actually written?

Such questions could go on and on, and with great profit. And asking such questions honestly — *as if you eagerly want to know the answers to them* — will have your mind and spirit working in the same direction with each other to find answers that relate directly for you. And you'll be surprised — *perhaps even amazed* — at how such questions will be (in a very good and exciting way) like new wine in old wineskins, ready to burst out of its dark confinement!

What's New?

Of course, this is not how Jesus used this imagery in Mt 9:17. He said it differently, like this:

οὐδὲ βάλλουσιν οἶνον **νέον** εἰς ἀσκοὺς παλαιούς· εἰ δὲ μή γε, ῥήγνυνται οἱ ἀσκοὶ καὶ ὁ οἶνος ἐκχεῖται καὶ οἱ ἀσκοὶ ἀπόλλυνται· ἀλλὰ βάλλουσιν οἶνον **νέον** εἰς ἀσκοὺς **καινούς**, καὶ ἀμφότεροι συντηροῦνται.

And no one pours **new** wine into old wineskins; otherwise the skins burst and the wine is spilled out and the skins are destroyed. Instead they put **new** wine into **new** wineskins and both are preserved." (NET)

I quote the NET Bible here to make a point: the word *new* is used three times in this verse. But looking at the Greek text above, it is clear that two different adjectives are used:

νέος, α, ον
καινός, ή, όν

You've already learned these as vocabulary words meaning "new." But in such a text as this, with both used together, this should *at least* cause you, as a disciplined reader, to ask: "Are these actually the same, or are they subtly different here?"

So then, if you look at English translations, you'll see this:

new/new/fresh ASV, NAS, RSV, NRSV, NJB, ESV, CSB, NAB

new/new/new KJV, NIV, NET, BBE, DBY, LEW, NGI, MIT

Right off, this tells you that at least some major translations treat the words νέος and καινός as mere synonyms and translate them the same. The other translations don't necessarily see them as different, but in an attempt to be contextually sensitive, and perhaps to provide some variety, they render them as *new* and *fresh*. Even these English words are often synonymous.

So from English translations, there does not appear to be very much difference, if any at all. And as a reader, you should respect such overwhelming views of professional translators. In fact, Friberg's Greek lexicon comes right out and says that νέος is "synonymous with καινός (MT 9.17)."[37]

So what else is there for *disciplined readers* to say on this?

New in Matthew

Well . . . let's not leave just yet. Let's ask whether Matthew's Gospel could be using these two words just a bit differently. Maybe not, and we don't want to *force* this. But maybe so, and if so, we don't want to *miss* this. So let us go searching.

First, νέος occurs twice in Matthew, both times of "new wine" and both times in this verse. However, καινός occurs four times in Matthew, never of wine. And even though it is properly translated as *new* or *fresh*, it appears every time to be pointing to something *qualitatively* new, beyond a simple meaning of *temporally* or *commonly* new or fresh.

9:17 "*new* wineskins" (also in Mk 2:22; Lk 5:38)
13:52 "*new* things and old things"
26:29 "I drink it *new* with you in the K" (also in Mk 14:25)
27:60 "placed him in his own *new* tomb" (also in Jn 19:41)

So in Matthew, *new wineskins* are more than just goatskins made for wine, they are the cloak with which we wrap ourselves as we

---

[37] Friberg 2000. Something BDAG does not do.

listen to Jesus' teachings. To drink it *new* with you does not merely mean *again*; it portends the complete newness of all in the Kingdom. And the *new tomb* in Matthew is not merely a tomb no one has used; it is *rich-man-Joseph's* new tomb, fulfilling Isa 53:4, 9, following up on and completing the direct quote of that text in Mt 8:17 (found only in Matthew). [38]

New in Isaiah

Ah, speaking of Isaiah, we come to our second point: The word νέος is used in Isaiah only for *new wine* (49:26) and *young children* (40:30; 65:20). However, καινός is used 13 times in Isaiah, all in very special texts:[39]

8:1	"a *new* large scroll" (for the words of κύριος)
41:15	Israel has been made "*new*, sharp, and with teeth."
42:9	"former things are past; I (κύριος v. 8) now say *new things* (καινὰ)[40]"
42:10	"a *new* song"
43:19	"I (κύριος v. 6) am doing *new things* (καινὰ)!"
48:6	"I (κύριος v. 2) will make you hear *new things* (καινὰ) that are about to happen, things you did not speak."
61:4	"they will *make new* the deserted cities" (a verb, here)
62:2	"he shall call you by your *new name*, which ὁ κύριος will name."
65:15-17	"to those who serve him, a *new* name shall be given, [16] which shall be blessed on the earth; for they shall bless the true God, and those who swear on the earth shall swear by the true God, for they shall forget their

[38] It is a great temptation to jump into the similarities and differences in all of the Gospels on this point, but space (and the purposes of this pre-grammar) prevents that. I will simply say that the detailed manner in which Matthew's Gospel develops this story highlights subtly the *new wineskins* more than Mark or Luke; and also that the use of καινός in Matthew is more refined than the others. The Johannine literature also reflects a special interest in καινός Jn. 13:34; 19:41; 1 Jn. 2:7, 8; 2 Jn. 1:5; Rev. 2:17; 3:12; 5:9; 14:3; 21:1, 2, 5; and in not using νέος but once (Jn 21:18), and that to mean younger person.

[39] These are my own translations of the LXX (the Greek Isaiah), because Matthew usually quotes from the Greek texts, not Hebrew.

[40] I merely point out here that the exact form found in Mt 13:53 for "new things" is in Isa 48:6.

first affliction, and it shall not come up into their heart. [17] For the heaven will be *new* and the earth will be *new* also, and they shall not remember the former things, nor shall they come upon their heart"

66:22   "For as the *new* heaven and the *new* earth, which I am making, remain before me, says κύριος, so shall your offspring and your name stand."

My point is that **in Isaiah, νέος and καινός both mean *new*; but they don't mean the same thing.** To compare *new wine* with the *new song*, or *new heaven and earth*, or *the new things* κύριος *is doing* would be reading without paying attention.[41]

Matthew Again

Does anyone here think that Matthew has read Isaiah? Time does not allow me to draw this out, but I suggest that more than the other Gospels, Matthew specifically calls upon this prophetic view of *new* for his own Gospel: Jesus is the new Moses; his teachings, the new Torah; those who follow him, the new scribes; his Kingdom, the new rule; and more. And yet he says this:

Μὴ νομίσητε ὅτι ἦλθον καταλῦσαι τὸν νόμον ἢ τοὺς προφήτας· οὐκ ἦλθον καταλῦσαι ἀλλὰ πληρῶσαι.

Don't think I came to destroy the Torah or the Prophets; I came not to destroy, but to make full! (Mt 5:17)

The *new things* are precious and exciting and breath-taking and wonderful! But they do not eliminate the *old things*, and every scribe trained for the Kingdom of heaven brings them *both* out of the treasure!

The bottom line? Matthew appears to be doing something more than simply using νέος and καινός synonymously. To translate them both as new may be perfectly fine. But by paying

---

[41] If anyone complains that it is not the word *new* that shows this, but the attached word (*wine, song, heaven, things*), the text itself will cry out against that complaint. The writers themselves showed this distinction: (1) New (νέος) *wine* only occurs in the these texts: Isa 49:26; Sir 9:10; Mt 9:17; Mk 2:22; Lk 5:37, 38 and the word is never καινός. (2) New (καινός) *wineskins* only occurs in these texts: Jos. 9:13; Mt 9:17; Mk 2:22; Lk 5:38 and the word is never νέος.

closer attention we see how Matthew may be using καινός in a prophetic sense, to bring a special emphasis to Jesus as Messiah.

I hasten to add that my argument here is about what is going on inside of the Gospel of Matthew. There are other uses of νέος and καινός that I have not talked about. Matthew appears to be more nuanced, whereas Mark and Luke do seem to use the words more interchangeably. (See Mk 1:27; 2:21, 22; 14:25; 16:17; and especially Lk 5:36, 38; 22:20.) This raises an important point about Greek word meanings: *Just because a word is used to mean something in one document does not give us the right to force that usage on other documents.* They might be the same; and they might be very different. We also did not talk about any occurrences in Paul, Hebrews, the General Letters, or John here.

Learning Greek

Matthew says it boldly: God is doing something *new* (in the prophetically loaded sense of the word) in what Jesus does and what he teaches. Anyone who attaches to Jesus as follower and disciplined learner will embrace this truth. Thinking about the context of this Gospel: if you approach Jesus' message bringing only your old, confined, dying self, you will hear but not hear what is in store for you as a student of Greek.

Now certainly, Matthew is not talking about learning Greek — and the point is not that NT Greek is the key to solving the world's problems. But can anyone doubt the value of learning Greek for exploring the meaning of even a single word? More than a single word, there is a principle here: *Approach Greek as a dead language for merely academic reasons, and that is very likely how you will use it and what you will get from it. But wrap yourself in a spirit of anticipation for what it can do for you spiritually — as a means of disciplining not just your mind, but your spiritual awareness and sensitivity — and you can count on a very spiritually stimulating result.*

CONSIDER THE SPIRIT IN YOU

Take up your journal and write about your favorite take-away from this chapter so far? Is there anything from this study that says *new* will be easy?

TIME FOR GREEK: ADJECTIVES (2)

VOCABULARY

ὅστις	"who, whoever" (pronoun)
πᾶς, πᾶσα, πᾶν	"all, every" (adjective)

Some easy adjectives:

κακός, -ή, -ον	"bad" (*cac*ophony)
πρῶτος, -η, -ον	"first" (*proto*type)
σοφός, -ή, -όν	"wise" (*soph*isticated; *soph*ist)
πιστός, -ή, -όν	"faithful"

MORE ABOUT ADJECTIVES

Reminder from last week:

Ἐγώ εἰμι ὁ [**καλός**] ποιμήν.
I am   the   good   shepherd.

A Fun Example from Jude 3

τῇ   [**ἅπαξ παραδοθείσῃ τοῖς ἁγίοις**] πίστει
for the once for all   having been delivered   to the   saints   faith
= *for the faith having once for all been delivered to the saints*

Notice how *the faith* has an adjectival clause telling what kind of faith it is: a "once-for-all-having-been-delivered-to-the-saints" faith.

Adjective as Noun (a substantive)

An adjective, when it does not modify a noun, can itself be used as a noun (a substantive), just like in English: "The good, the bad, and the ugly." So if you find an adjective by itself, not modifying a noun, it is most likely a substantive:

καινός ἐστιν ἐκ θεοῦ. "**A new man** is from God."
καινή ἐστιν ἐκ θεοῦ. "**A new woman** is from God."
καινόν ἐστιν ἐκ θεοῦ. "**A new thing** is from God."

ὁ καινός ἐστιν ἐκ θεοῦ. "**The new man** is from God."
ἡ καινή ἐστιν ἐκ θεοῦ. "**The new woman** is from God."
τὸ καινόν ἐστιν ἐκ θεοῦ. "**The new thing** is from God."

ἐκβάλλει **καινὰ** "he/she brings out **new things**"
ἐκβάλλει **τὰ καινὰ** "he/she brings out **the new things**"

We have looked at only two uses of the adjective:

1. As an attributive
2. As a substantive

There is much more to know about adjectives. But this is all we need for our purposes in looking specifically at Mt 13:52.

TRANSLATE THIS

1. ὁ καινὸς ἄνθρωπος ἐκβάλλει καινὰ καὶ

   παλαιὰ ἐκ τοῦ καινοῦ θησαυροῦ τῆς βασιλείας

   τῶν οὐρανῶν.

2. ὁ παλαιὸς ἄνθρωπος ἐκβάλλει τὰ παλαιὰ ἐκ τῆς

   παλαιᾶς βασιλείας.

DISCIPLINE YOURSELF

This chapter gives more on how Greek adjectives work.

1. Learn the **vocabulary**.

2. **Translate** the sentences above.

3. Make sure you understand what the chapter is showing you about how adjectives work. You don't need to memorize them. Don't fret if it is strange to you. Go over the examples.

4. Keep reviewing the **article chart**.

TRANSLATION KEY

(for the sentences above on the previous page)

1. *"The new man brings out new things and old things from the new treasure of the Kingdom of Heaven."*

    ὁ καινὸς ἄνθρωπος is all nom sg subject (look at the article);

    καινά and παλαιά are adjectives used like nouns (substantives) and are both neuter plural.

    ἐκ τοῦ καινοῦ θησαυροῦ is a prepositional phrase, all in the genitive case (because ἐκ requires a gen case). Notice that the article and adjective agree with the noun in cgn (case, gender, number).

    τῆς βασιλείας τῶν οὐρανῶν Two articular nouns (= nouns with articles); the first is sg, the second pl. Technically, the second modifies the first, and the first (τῆς βασιλείας) modifies θησαυροῦ: "treasure *of* the Kingdom *of* the Heavens. This indicates some kind of relationship, such as "a treasure *belonging to* the K/H" or *"deriving from"* etc.

2. *"The old man brings/throws out the old things from the old kingdom."*

    All notes are virtually the same.

10
Old

The study of NT Greek can . . .
energize your spiritual interest.

GUIDE TEXT:

ὁ δὲ εἶπεν αὐτοῖς· διὰ τοῦτο πᾶς γραμματεὺς μαθητευθεὶς
And he said to them: "Because of this, every scribe who has been trained

τῇ βασιλείᾳ τῶν οὐρανῶν ὅμοιός ἐστιν ἀνθρώπῳ οἰκοδεσπότῃ,
for the Kingdom of Heaven   is like   a master of a household,

ὅστις ἐκβάλλει ἐκ τοῦ θησαυροῦ αὐτοῦ καινὰ   καὶ **παλαιά**.
who   brings out   from   his treasure   new things   and   **old (things).**

OLD

Whereas *new* can be exciting, *old* can be reassuring. It can offer wisdom and guidance, provide stability, and warn of danger. To keep an individual or organization from careening off the walls or into oblivion, what is tested and tried can ensure endurance and engender legacy. This is just as true of spiritual pursuits as of any other.

In the New Testament, when old and new are contrasted, *old* is normally negative. There are two main words:

ἀρχαῖος: "old, ancient" (**Mt 5:21, 33**; Lk 9:8, 19; Acts 15:7, 21; 21:16; 2Cor 5:17; 2Pet 2:5; Rev 12:9; 20:2)

παλαιός: "old, obsolete" (**Mt 9:16, 17; 13:52**; Mk 2:21, 22; Lk 5:36, 37, 39; Rom 6:6; 1Cor 5:7, 8; 2Cor 3:14; Eph 4:22; Col 3:9; 1Jn 2:7)

We note immediately that the definitions are only general, and that both words are used in Matthew. Our immediate questions, here, become *how are these words used* and *are they related?*

In the Bible Generally

When we look up each occurrence of these words in both the LXX[42] and NT texts, we get to see how the words were being used over a period of hundreds of years in a variety of texts. We then can write up a summary of how the words were used, much like our own dictionary entry. It would look something like this:

(1) ἀρχαῖος (adjective) tends to be used in texts that refer to (a) days or generations of old, ancient times, and the prophets of old[43]; (b) of first or original things[44]; (c) and even what God did prior to creation — the oldest of the old.[45]

(2) παλαιός (adjective) tends to be used in texts referring to (a) old age[46]; or (b) old food, people, places, events, things, and personal acquaintances[47]; or (c) of the old covenant[48]; or (d) in texts that imply obsolete and outdated things.[49]

These are general conclusions (hence the phrase, "tends to be"), and it is always important to apply meanings to specific texts that are suitable to or demanded by each individual context. That is to say, the distinctions offered above do not always apply to every text. (It is not legitimate for us simply to grab any definition we like.) E.g., ἀρχαῖος sometimes looks like a synonym of παλαιός. It is used of an old pool[50]; an old friend[51];

---

[42] We certainly want to look at how the words are used in the LXX since the old Greek translations were "the Bible" of the early church. Remember, the LXX (Septuagint) as we now have it includes the Greek OT + Greek Apocrypha.

[43] 1Sam 24:14; 1Ki 2:35; 5:10; 2Ma 6:22; Ps 43:2; 76:6; 78:8; 88:50; 138:5; 142:5; Wis 8:8; 13:10; Sir 2:10; 16:7; 39:1; Ps Sol 18:12; Isa 25:1; 43:18; Lam 1:7; 2:17; Mt 5:21, 33; Lk 9:8, 19; Acts 15:7, 21; 21:16; 2Cor 5:17; 2Pet 2:5; Rev 12:9; 20:2

[44] Ps 138:5; Ezek 21:21

[45] Isa 37:6

[46] e.g., "The Ancient of Days" in Dan 7:9, 13, 22

[47] Lev 25:22; 26:10; Jos 9:4, 5; 1Sam 7:12; Est 8:12; 2Ma 6:21; 3Ma 3:18; Cant 7:14; Job 15:10; Jer 45:11; Dan 7:9, 13, 22; Mt 9:16, 17; 13:52; Mk 2:21, 22; Lk 5:36, 37, 39; 1Jn 2:7

[48] 2Cor 3:14 (unfortunately translated "old testament" in the KJV)

[49] Rom 6:6; 1Cor 5:7, 8; Eph 4:22; Col 3:9; cf also the verb παλαιόω Dt 29:4; Josh 9:5, 13; Neh 9:21; and many others; also Heb 8:13

[50] Isa 22:9, 11

[51] Sir 9:10

a previous condition[52]; of something obsolete[53]; and also of "just a few years ago" (rather than an ancient time).[54] Even the adverb πάλαι "of old, long ago, from ancient times" shows a similar kind of flexibility, being used very much like ἀρχαῖος.[55]

To summarize, in any specific text, we might not be surprised if we find a general distinction between these two words (as indicated above). However, we must not *force* such a distinction on specific texts. In fact, the two words might be more similar than different in some texts.

In the New Testament

Looking more specifically at the NT: **Paul** never uses these words in a positive sense, always speaking of putting off the old man, old yeast, old covenant, or old creation. **Mark and Luke** only employ the words for old age or in contrast to what is new. Luke has the positive statement: "The old is good," but look more closely. This is not stated to show how good the old is, but rather in a list of things which spells out what no one in his right mind ever does. Namely, no one puts new wine into old skins, puts a new patch on an old garment, or drinks new wine when aged wine is available. The point in Luke is that nobody is daft enough to do those things. It is not that old skins, clothes, and wine are good; rather, this list shows why Jesus' disciples should not be stopped from feasting now: because it does not make sense (just like those other things make no sense). They can fast later. And finally, aside from the Synoptics and Paul, **a few texts** make a simple reference to the past, or to old age, or to some previous directive. [56]

---

[52] Isa 23:17

[53] Isa 43:18f = old vs new as replacement; see also 2Cor 5:17

[54] Acts 15:7; 21:16

[55] Est 3:13; 3Mac 4:1; Wis 11:14; 12:3, 27; Isa 37:26; 48:5, 7; **Mt 11:21**; Lk 10:13; Heb 1:1; Jude 1:4, including "of recent times" Mk 15:44; 2Cor 12:19; 2Pet 1:9

[56] Acts 15:7, 21; 21:16; 2Pt 2:5; 1Jn 2:7; Rev 12:9; 20:2

In Matthew

All of that now being said, we are in a position to see something that we might otherwise have missed. For something powerful takes place in Matthew; something subtle, but mountain-moving![57] In Mt 13:52—at the very end, at the very last word of the last of the eight parables—Jesus now mentions the word παλαιά ("old things"). Seems unexceptional.

But in the larger context of Matthew, there are two different kinds of old things: **(1)** *positively,* **those that come from God** (i.e., what God has said of old in the sacred writings and how those things might apply now in light of the new teachings of Jesus[58]), and **(2)** *negatively,* **those that come from the Pharisees** (i.e., for Matthew, the old, obsolete, and lifeless teachings that undermine and destroy the essence of God's old, old story. This is illustrated numerous times starting in the Sermon on the Mount in chapter 5,[59] escalating in the following chapters, and then culminating in chapter 23. It is also evident in the details of how Matthew tells the story of Jesus' trial 26:57ff, and also the guard at the tomb 27:62ff.)

By "two kinds of old," I do not mean that the key is in some supposed verbal distinctions between ἀρχαῖος (5:21, 33) and παλαιός (13:52). As a matter of fact, in Matthew these two words are working together to build a case *for* what God has said of old and *against* the longstanding tradition of the Pharisees. What God has done of old is not now being dispensed with; it is rather being filled to the full. The two different kinds of old things are theologically identified and set forward by Matthew's entire

---

[57] Especially relevant for Matthew, occurring twice (17:20 and 21:21), compared to only once in Mk 11:23, and not at all in Luke or John.

[58] Cf. Hagner 2000, 402 "not merely new hermeneutical applications of the Torah in new situations . . . nor new applications of old sayings of Jesus, . . . but the relation of the Torah to the genuinely new reality of the Kingdom of God."

[59] The statements "you have heard that it was said, but I say to you" in Mt 5:21, 27, 33, 38, 43 are not Jesus against the Law (against Guelich 1982, 175ff, esp. 184). Rather, these are against a strictly casuistic (legal) application of the laws which take no account of the intent of the laws.

Gospel. They are concerned with the *source, nature, quality, and value of what is old*, not with the *fact* of being old.

To state this another way, in Matthew, a *Jesus-disciple*—a scribe trained for the Kingdom—must know the difference between the two. They must know which old things to bring out, and which old things to leave behind, and how all such things work with the new teachings of Jesus about the Kingdom of Heaven.

So once again (as in a previous chapter) we might rightly translate our words as "old." But that really is not enough. In Matthew's context, it is not simply a reference to what happened a long time ago. These words are now used to underscore the good (from God) that must be kept, and the bad (from how people continually corrupt it) that must be left behind.

CONSIDER THE SPIRIT IN YOU

Now take out your journal and write. This will be the last journal entry that I ask you to make. Thinking about the previous four pages:

1. Describe whether the previous pages are merely academic for you or are also spiritually valuable. Be as specific as you can be.

2. Evaluate in writing the following sentence. What attracts or repels you about it? *Such study can open doors that before were completely hidden from view, and they can help focus on key issues in texts that otherwise might not even be noticed. They might even help us identify some old things that we keep in our treasure room that we should throw out. That fact alone makes this worth our time.*

TIME FOR GREEK:
NEXT STEPS & RESOURCES

CONGRATULATIONS

Congratulations! You have arrived at the end of this course! From the very first page of this book, I have been talking about *why* NT Greek should be pursued as a spiritual discipline, and *how* the small amount of Greek I've presented is merely a "jump start" into the language. Hopefully, by now, you realize that this marvelous step you have taken is only **Step 1**.

NEXT STEPS

It is natural to take a short break after any step. However, it is important not to allow what you've learned to grow cold. Here I will talk briefly about what's next. **Step 2** (vocabulary learning) and especially **Step 3** (a deeper study of the language) will help you on this path of a truly *spiritual* discipline.

To see all 4 Steps, go to this link:
BiblicalConversation.com/GreekHome3

Here I will address some important concerns for you about any next steps you might choose to make.

1. **Solo:** Although it is possible to learn NT Greek *all by yourself,* most people find this difficult. It takes a tremendous amount of self-starting and study discipline to learn a language alone.

2. **Credit:** If you want *college credit*, make sure you know why. A degree or a profession is a good reason. Otherwise, it is a mistake to think that an accredited course necessarily translates into higher (or even high) quality. It might, but it might not.[60] Quality and value depend mainly on the one teaching the course, the text used, the schedule, the personal

---

[60] While a needed practice overall, accrediting rules are designed for institutional agendas with federal funding needs. As such, they can override or overlook needs of specific courses or classes. For example, ACICS (in the bibliography) applies *quality* five times to institutional, not course, goals. Also, see Broken 2017 which calls out the current accreditation system.

attention available to you, whether you have ongoing access to the material, cost, and more.

3. **Online Greek:** Although a physical classroom has some advantages, it cannot ensure you'll get more attention or better instruction. *High quality recorded (and sometimes "live") classes are available online.* Be choosy about what online group you connect with. I recommended all of the following:

a) Patrick Spicer and Gary D. Collier offer a full year of beginning Greek followed by a live and active weekly Greek NT Translation Team (GNT3). (1) **The full year of Greek** has 39 lessons with 58 hours of detailed video instruction designed for new, busy, and/or working people. The course is based on the grammar by David Black who has given his strong recommendation for this course. This course is recorded and comes with live email based help for all recorded sessions. It also comes with proprietary apps and tools for vocabulary, word formation, and more. Occasionally the class is re-offered "live." (2) **The GNT3** is not a class but an ongoing week-by-week translation team, working its way through the NT and some LXX documents. A monthly donation is requested, and you have *lifetime access* to all materials covered without additional cost.
BiblicalConversation.com/Step3 Full Year of Greek
BiblicalConversation.com/Step4 Translation team

b) Robert Plummer, "Learn Biblical Greek" in 26 lessons and with about 10-12 hours of video, based on the grammar by David Black. *There is no cost.* Quality videos are brief and to the point; excellent for reference and review. Also free is *The Daily Dose of Greek* which is just what it says and well worth a few minutes each day. Additional online helps and videos are also available. This is a great and trustworthy resource, especially for busy people who want to touch Greek daily.
DailyDoseOfGreek.com/Learn-Biblical-Greek/

c) William Mounce offers a full version of Greek and a less comprehensive "Greek for the Rest of Us." The full version is based on the 4th edition of Mounce's own excellent grammar and workbook, and the course has 37 lessons and about 19 hours of high quality video. Both versions include online helps. There is a cost for both with a possible annual renewal option, and a smaller free version. This is very high quality website and material. Courses.ZondervanAcademic.com/Biblical-Greek

d) Mark Dubis and Nicholas Ellis at Bible Mesh offer three classes with about 40 lessons. There is a cost for each and an annual or so renewal. Hours of video not disclosed. Courses.Biblemesh.com/ (look for Greek Courses)

In all cases, one should only enter a Greek course knowing *how much time* will be required each week, *how much effort* you will commit to, and *how much actual help* you will receive outside of recordings. This is a big deal! As mentioned above, learning solo sounds good, but most soon discover they crave "live" help. Also, *how long you get access to your course* is important, because once you take a class, you will likely want to have ongoing access to that material (videos, etc.), even years later. It is not unusual for students who have had Greek to want to go through that course, or parts of it, again.

Avoid thinking that once you have "taken a course" you're done. Always keep in mind your determination to walk daily into a disciplined use of Greek for your spiritual growth and benefit.

MAJOR GREEK TOOLS & RESOURCES

Now let's talk about some important Greek resources. These are based on the website found at:

BibleDashboard.com
click on *The Greek Help Center*

You are encouraged to look over that site. Its aim is to provide practical guidance for selected resources for both new students and those growing in their Greek reading proficiency.

NT Greek Manuscripts and Editions

Today, there are 5,686 Greek manuscripts (either in whole or pieces) of the NT from the 2nd to the 16th centuries.

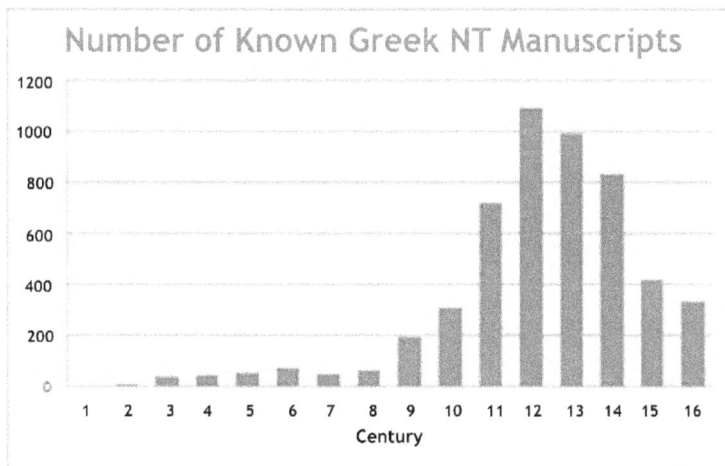

Number of Known Greek NT Manuscripts

Table 8
From Patheos website via Wikipedia

All printed Greek New Testaments today are "composite" editions. This means that they are not based on any one Greek manuscript from antiquity, but on the critical evaluation of thousands. They are made by examining available Greek manuscripts and by attempting to reconstruct the earliest Greek texts possible. The science of manuscript examination and evaluation is called *textual criticism*. Scholars from all over the world engage in this study. One leading center in the United States is *The Center for the Study of NT Manuscripts* in Plano, TX. (http://www.csntm.org/)

Essentially, current Greek editions are of three kinds:

1. **A "Critical Text"**: The two best known are the NA28 (Nestle-Aland 28th ed.) and UBS4 (United Bible Society 4th ed.). Also available are the SBL Greek NT and the Greek NT produced at Tyndale House, Cambridge.

2. **The Majority Text**: This approach adds up all manuscript variants and goes with the majority. A small (but vocal) minority advocates this or the next.

3. **Textus Receptus**: This is the text on which the KJV was based. Often, this is mistaken for the second (above), but they are different. These have value, but you should be wary of anyone insisting that "the real" Greek NT is either #2 or #3.

Greek Texts: Interlinears

An interlinear is like a set of training wheels for students who are not yet able to ride on their own. We've been using an example of one throughout this book:

ὁ δὲ εἶπεν αὐτοῖς· διὰ τοῦτο πᾶς γραμματεὺς μαθητευθεὶς
And he said to them: "Because of this, every scribe who has been trained

τῇ βασιλείᾳ τῶν οὐρανῶν ὅμοιός ἐστιν ἀνθρώπῳ οἰκοδεσπότῃ,
for the Kingdom of Heaven　　　is like　　a master of a household,

ὅστις ἐκβάλλει ἐκ τοῦ θησαυροῦ αὐτοῦ καινὰ　　καὶ　παλαιά.
who brings out from his treasure　　new things and　old.

The English translation listed under each word is one possible gloss[61] by the editor. For example, in the text above at the end of line 2 are the words

ἀνθρώπῳ οἰκοδεσπότῃ
a master of a household

More literally, this might be translated in these ways: "a man, a householder" or "a person, a householder" or even "one who is a householder" or just "householder" or "household manager."

Much more could be said about this, but the point here is that an interlinear (whether in a book or software) gives a **bald Greek text** and a **possible gloss** for the word above it. Some will also put **codes** beneath each word to help identify the word. Even so, the actual work of determining the text, the grammatical

---

[61] A possible meaning of the word. Words always have a range of meanings depending on context. E.g., for *story*, glosses would be "a tale, a floor, or a lie."

structure, its function in the context, the range of meanings of words, a suitable translation, and the like are not provided by an interlinear. All of that must be supplied by readers who have experience with the language on a more intimate basis. Hence, as training wheels, an interlinear

1. provides a Greek text so you can practice reading it out loud;

2. can help you read your English Bibles, especially when doing word studies;

3. can help keep you interested when learning Greek.

An *interlinear New Testament* can be a handy tool for a beginner. The biggest mistake beginning Greek students make is to use an interlinear in a paint-by-numbers fashion, as if it shows "what the Greek *really* says." If you need to use an interlinear text, that's fine — there is no shame in learning to ride. But use it all the while being aware of the limitations.

Concordance

Besides the Greek text itself, a Greek or Greek-English concordance (whether a book or software) is *the most important New Testament study tool that you have.* Used properly, you can look up for yourself how words are used in various contexts. I have been demonstrating this very thing throughout this book.

Please hear my encouragement to graduate from Strong's *Exhaustive Concordance* as early as you can. Use the Greek you've learned to get away from such resources. Besides, using Kohlenberger's *Greek-English Concordance* is far easier and more accurate. Better still is his *The Exhaustive Concordance to the Greek New Testament.* Finally, I also recommend a small concordance to carry with you: Schmoller's *Handkonkordanz Zum Griechischen (English and German Edition.* But beware, the English here is only in the introduction.

Of course, the very best concordance tool is in Bible software (like Accordance or Logos). There is no better way to search a Greek text than electronically.

Lexicons

Lexicons (dictionaries) tell you *how words get used* more than what they *must mean*. (There's a difference—words almost always have a range of meanings, depending on context.) Lexicons are compiled by documenting how words are used in a variety of texts. Words might change "meanings" over time or in different circumstances. E.g., in English, "nice" was used in the 14th century to mean "wanton or dissolute." It now tends to be used to indicate "polite or kind." *A lexicon charts usage; it does not dictate meaning.*

Greek Lexicons range from short to comprehensive. Here are two of the better known lexicons.

1. Thayer's

You may hear about Thayer's *Greek Lexicon* as though it is the best one to use. That was once true, but Thayer himself would not use it now. It is out of date, and sometimes wrong. Save your money, you can get it free. It is far better than the tiny dictionary in the back of Strong's, so if Thayer's is all you have, it will work.

2. BDAG

BDAG 3rd edition is the best NT lexicon available. It is pricey, but the best. "BDAG" stands for the names of the authors. This is the standard scholarly lexicon today. I would not recommend buying this unless you are going to be doing some heavy research. But if you have access to it, this is the one to use. You can get inside of good Bible software, but you might pay extra.

ONLINE GREEK HELPS

Again, I strongly urge you to go to the following link and spend some time looking around:

BibleDashboard.com
Select *The Greek Help Center.*

Once on that site, look especially for the following:

1. **The 5 Major Areas of Greek Help**

   a. Online Helps for Learning Greek
   b. The 7 Book Starter Set
   c. Bible Software that uses Greek and Hebrew
   d. How to do Word Studies
   e. Books on Greek

2. **Bible Software**

   a. Free: **Lumina** and **ESword**
   b. Premium: **Accordance** or **Logos**
   (Both are heavy duty)
   c. Word Processing: a program called **Nota Bene**

DISCIPLINE YOURSELF

All the King's horses
and all the King's men
cannot make you do one thing more
with Greek ever again.

It *really is* up to you. If you choose a Greek path, remember: *Every English speaker and reader who has ever learned NT Greek started out not knowing any more than you do right now.*

This book has neither claimed nor suggested that NT Greek is required for all or even most Christians. Hardly. What it has claimed is that *a life-long pursuit of NT Greek as a spiritual discipline can bless anyone who decides to walk that path.* This book (1) has offered seven major benchmarks for how Greek can bless you spiritually; (2) it has spent a good deal of time demonstrating those benchmarks by walking through one text: Mt 13:52; and (3) it has offered you a taste of the Greek language itself without overloading you with too much technical detail.

So then, knowing that you have now completed Step 1,[62] I hope to do something (right now) as *radically personable as it is*

---

[62] To see all 4 Steps, go to BiblicalConversation.com/GreekHome3

unusual. Indeed, allow me now to step out from behind this written text to ask you a question face to face:

How would you say that the scribe which Jesus spoke about in Mt 13:52 relates to you right now, today?

Only you can answer this for yourself. I cannot prescribe this for you or for anyone else.

But I *can* answer this for myself. For me personally, this text (Mt 13:52) has been for many years — and it remains — a calling to *read the Bible like Jesus.* And the study of Greek is a crucial part of this. Far more than an academic subject, NT Greek has deepened my spiritual resolve that the texts we have received are the most precious in the world.

I want to repeat this, because I want to be crystal clear about it. So I'm going set this statement apart:

*The spiritual resolve that inspires, enlivens, and motivates me does not arise because of (1) any ecclesiastical doctrine or (2) any academic rule about the nature of biblical texts or (3) any faith statement I have to sign to keep a job. Such a resolve comes rather from spending time in the texts themselves, from roaming through the words, the phrases, the idioms, and the intertextual realities of these texts, as if strolling breathless-in-wonder through wooded gardens. **That** is what inspires me to view the Bible as I do and to teach it as I do.*

Hanging on every paragraph, sentence, and word is neither a legalistic requirement nor an exercise in vanity. Instead, it is a joy and a pleasure — it's an incredible privilege — that in our time we have such precious ancient texts and such an opportunity to walk around in them. I said it in the very first chapter:

I never feel closer to God than when I am walking around neck-deep in a biblical Greek text!

This is what being a scribe trained for the Kingdom of Heaven means to me. It is a spiritual quest, but not always an easy path. It sometimes means making sacrifices in time by giving up less-meaningful activities. It certainly requires discipline — and discipline does not always feel good. But the results far surpass any pain in the moment.

Two biblical texts say this most beautifully:

ὁ ἀγαπῶν **παιδείαν**	*The one who loves **discipline***
ἀγαπᾷ αἴσθησιν	*loves learning,*
ὁ δὲ μισῶν ἐλέγχους	*but the one who hates being tested*
ἄφρων	*is not thinking straight!*

Prov 12:1 BGT/GDC

πᾶσα δὲ **παιδεία** . . .	*Discipline . . .*
οὐ δοκεῖ χαρᾶς εἶναι	*It never seems like joy,*
ἀλλὰ λύπης	*just pain!*
ὕστερον δὲ	*It is only later,*
καρπὸν εἰρηνικὸν	*as a delightful end-result*
τοῖς δι᾽ αὐτῆς	*for those who through it*
γεγυμνασμένοις	*have been trained,*
ἀποδίδωσιν	*that the payoff comes:*
δικαιοσύνης	*You are set right!*

Heb 12:11 BGT/GDC

Appendix

1.
Vocabulary

Following is an alphabetic index to the 30+ vocab words presented in this book.

ἄνθρωπος, -ου, ὁ	"a person, a human, a man"	44, 54, 78
αὐτός	"he" (αὐτοῦ ="of him"; αὐτοῖς ="to them"	54
βασιλεία -ας, ἡ	"kingdom	54, 78
γραμματεύς, έως, ο	"scribe, lawyer, expert in the law"(cf. English *grammatical*)	38, 78
διὰ τοῦτο	"because of this" (preposition + adj)	76
ἐγώ	"I" (emphatic form pronoun)	76
εἰμι	"I am"	76
εἶπεν	"he said"; see the phrase ὁ δὲ εἶπεν	38
ἐκ	"out, out of, from" (preposition)	44
ἐκβάλλω	"I cast out, I bring out"	44
ἔστιν	"he (or she or it) is" (3ʳᵈ sg of εἰμι above, p. 76)	38
εὐαγγέλιον, -ου, τό	"gospel, good news"	76, 78
θεός, -ου, ὁ	"God"	64, 78
θησαυρός, -ου, ὁ	"treasure, storehouse" (English *thesaurus*)	64, 78
καί	"and"	38
καινός, -ή, -όν	"new"	89
κακός, -ή, -όν	"bad" (*caco*phony)	101
καλός, -ή, -όν	"good, beautiful"	89
κύριος, -ου, ὁ	"Lord, master"	64, 78
λόγος, -ου, ὁ	"the word"	38, 78
λύω	"I loose, release, set free"	44
μαθητεύω	"I disciple, teach, train, school."	44
νεός, -ά, -όν	"new" (*neo*natal)	89
ὁ δὲ εἶπεν	"and he said"	38
ὁ, ἡ, τό	"the"	76
οἰκοδεσπότης, -ου, ὁ	"household manager, householder, manager of a house"	64, 78
ὅμοιος, οία, ον	"like"	89
ὅστις	"who, whoever"	101
οὐρανός, -ου, ὁ	"heaven, sky"	54, 78
παλαιός -ά, -όν	"old"	89
πᾶς, πᾶσα, πᾶν	"all, every"	101
πιστός, -ή, -όν	"faithful"	101
πρῶτος, -η, -ον	"first" (*proto*type)	101
σοφός, -ή, -όν	"wise" (*sophi*sticated; *soph*ist)	101

2.
Resources Used or Quoted

Standard Greek Texts & Grammars

Many Greek reference tools were used over the years while developing, teaching, and writing this material through several major drafts (1998, 2002, 2011, 2015, 2018, 2019). Instead of listing those references here, please go to:

BD   BibleDashboard.com click on "Greek Helps"
                and look under "More Greek Books."

Spiritual Disciplines

de Sales n.d.   De Sales, Francis. *Introduction to a Devout Life*. Aeterna Press. n.d. and no page numbers.

Foster 1998   Foster, Richard. *Celebration of Discipline* 2nd ed. Harper, 1978, rev. 1988, 1998.

Merton 1969   Thomas Merton, *Contemplative Prayer*. Doubleday, 1969.

Willard 1988   Willard, Dallas. *The Spirit of the Disciplines: Understanding How God Changes Lives*. Harper-Collins, 1988.

Willard 1998   Willard, Dallas. *The Divine Conspiracy: Rediscovering Our Hidden Life In God*. Harper-Collings, 1998.

Whitney 2014   Whitney, Don. *Spiritual Disciplines for the Christian Life*. 1991 revised 2014.

Whitney 2015   Whitney, Don. Live interview online: "What are Spiritual Disciplines" https://www.desiringgod.org/interviews/what-are-spiritual-disciplines Dec 2015 (accessed May 2019)

General Scripture

Collier 1994   Collier, Gary D. "'That We Might Not Crave Evil': The Structure and Argument of 1 Corinthians 10:1-13." *JSNT* 55 (1994) 55-75.

Collier 2012   Collier, Gary D. *Scripture, Canon, & Inspiration. Faith in Search of Conversation*. CWP Press, 2012.

Collier 2015   Collier, Gary D. *Unrelenting Faith*. Volume 1: *What Really Matters*. Vol 2: *Rising above Struggle, Walking in Hope*.

1Thessalonians, Conversations 1-20. CCAP. The Dialogē Press, 2015 (each volume with Journals).

Collier 2018a   Collier, Gary D. *"I, Paulos": Shades of Conversation in 1Thessalonians – An Odyssey of Authors and Texts, and of Reading Paul Conversationally.* The Dialogē Press. 2017 (corrected edition, April 2018).

Collier 2018b   Collier, Gary D. *Shades of Biblical Conversation: The Art of Conversing with Biblical Authors.* The Dialogē Press, 2018.

Collier 2018c   Collier, Gary D. *Graphē in Biblical and Related Literature. Is the Term* Scripture *an Appropriate Translation in English Bibles?* The Dialogē Press, 2018.

Hagner 2012   Hagner, Donald A. *The New Testament: A Historical and Theological Introduction.* Baker Academic, 2012.

Friberg 2000   Friberg, Timothy and Barbara. *Analytical Lexicon to the Greek New Testament.* 1994, 2000.

Jobes 2015   Jobes, H. and Silva, Moisés. *Invitation to the Septuagint.* 2nd Edition. Baker Academic, 2015.

Robertson 1915   Robertson, A. T. "The Language of the New Testament." *ISBE*, 1915. Now available online at http://www.bible-researcher.com/language-nt.html. This article was not, unfortunately, kept in the Revised ISBE alongside the newer article.

Gospel of Matthew

Blomberg 1992   Blomberg, Craig. *Matthew.* The New American Commentary. Broadman, 1992.

Chouinard 1997   Chouinard, Larry. *Matthew.* College Press, 1997.

Collier 1993   Collier, Gary D. *The Forgotten Treasure: Reading the Bible Like Jesus.* Howard, 1993.

D&A 2004   Davies, W. D., and Allison, Dale C. *Matthew.* ICC. 3 volumes. T & T Clark, Bloomsbury, 1997. 3rd edition 2004.

France 2007   France, R. T. *The Gospel of Matthew.* NICNT. Eerdmans, 2007.

Guelich 1982   Guelich, Robert A. *The Sermon on the Mount: A Foundation for Understanding.* Word Books, 1982.

Gundry 1994   Gundry, Robert H. *Matthew: A Commentary on His Handbook for a Mixed Church under Persecution.* 2nd edition. 1988. 1998.

Hagner 2000	Hagner, Donald A. *Matthew 1-13 vol 33A*. Word Biblical Commentary. Zondervan, 2000.
Keener 2009	Keener, Craig. *The Gospel of Matthew: A Socio-Rhetorical Commentary*. Eerdmans, 1999; 2009.
Kingsbury 1969	Kingsbury, Jack D. *The Parables of Jesus in Matthew 13: A Study in Redaction-Criticism*. SPCK, 1969.
Kingsbury 1988	Kingsbury, Jack D. *Matthew as Story*. 2nd edition. Fortress, 1988.
Kingsbury 1991	Kingsbury, Jack D. *Matthew: Structure, Christology, Kingdom*. Augsburg, 1991.
Lewis 1976	Lewis, Jack P. *The Gospel According to Matthew. 2 volumes*. Sweet, 1976.
Vorster 1977	W.S. Vorster. *The Structure of Matthew 1-13: An Exploration Into Discourse Analysis*. Neotestamentica Vol. 11:1977, 130-138. Available online at JSTOR: https://www.jstor.org/stable/43048976
Wenham 1979	Wenham, David. "The Structure of Matthew XIII." *NTS* 25(1978-79): 516-22.
Wilkens 1988	Wilkens, Michael J. *The Concept of Disciple in Matthew's Gospel*. Leiden: E. J. Brill, 1988.

Websites

Greek Online Resources

4 Steps	*4 Steps to a Life with Greek* BiblicalConversation.com/GreekHome/
BC	BiblicalConversation.com *or* CoffeeWithPaul.com
BD	Lists numerous select resources BibleDashboard.com
BG	*Mounce Biblical Greek Courses* Courses.ZondervanAcademic.com/Biblical-Greek
BibMesh	Courses.Biblemesh.com
CSNTM	*The Center for the Study of NT Manuscripts* CSMTM.org
CWP	CoffeeWithPaul.com *or* BiblicalConversation.com
DDG	*Plummer Greek Courses and Resources* DailyDoseOfGreek.com

IABC	*Institute for the Art of Biblical Conversation* BiblicalConversation.com
Robertson 1915	"The Language of the New Testament." ISBE, 1915. Bible-Researcher.com/language-nt.html

Other Online Resources

ACICS	"Importance of Accreditation." Accrediting Council for Independent Colleges and Schools http://www.acics.org/students/content.aspx?id=4320
Broken 2017	"Accreditation is Broken. Time to Repair It." *The Chronicle of Higher Education.* May 30, 2017. https://www.chronicle.com/article/Accreditation-Is-Broken-Time/240086
Wallace 2014	DanielWallace.com

Word Study Fallacies

The following are listed because a good portion of this present book is given to word studies of varying complexity.

Barr 1961	Barr, James. *Semantics of Biblical Language.* Oxford, 1961.
Black 1995	Black, David A. *Linguistics for Students of New Testament Greek: A Survey of Basic Concepts and Applications.* Baker, 1995. Page 125.
Carson 1996	Carson, D. A. *Exegetical Fallacies.* Baker Academic, 1996.
Plummer	Plummer, Robert "Illegitimate Totality Transfer, word study fallacy 3" https://vimeo.com/133111562
Wallace 2014	Wallace, Daniel. "Lexical Fallacies by Linguists" https://danielbwallace.com/tag/illegitimate-totality-transfer/
Wilkin 1989	Wilkin, Robert N. "Repentance and Salvation: Part 3: New Testament Repentance: Lexical Considerations" https://faithalone.org/journal/1989ii/Wilkin.html

3.
Abbreviations

Following on the next few pages . . .

English Translations of the Bible

English Translations from BibleWorks

ASV   American Standard Version (1901)
BBE   The Bible in Basic English (1949/64)
CEB   Common English Bible
CJB   Complete Jewish Bible
CSB   Holman Christian Standard Bible
CSB17 Holman Christian Standard Bible 2017
DBY   The Darby Bible (1884/1890)
DRA   The Douay-Rheims 1899 American Edition
ERV   English Revised Version (1885)
ESV   The English Standard Version (2007)
ETH   The Etheridge NT English Peshitta (1849)
GNV   Geneva (1599)
GWN   God's Word to the Nations Translation
JPS   Jewish Publication Society OT (1917)
KJA   King James (1611) Apocrypha
KJG   King James Version with Geneva Notes
KJV   King James (1611/1769) with Codes
LEW   The Lewis NT English Peshitta (1896)
LXA   LXX English Translation with Apocrypha (Brenton)
LXE   LXX English Translation (Brenton)
MGI   The Magiera NT English Peshitta (2006)
MIT   MacDonald Idiomatic Translation
MRD   The Murdock NT English Peshitta (1851)
NAB   The New American Bible
NAS   New American Standard Bible (1977) with Codes
NAU   New American Standard Bible (1995) with Codes
NET   The Net Bible
NETS   New English Translation of the LXX
NIB   New International Version (BR)
NIBO   New International Version (BR 1984)
NIrV   New International Readers Version
NIV   New International Version (1984) (US)
NJB   The New Jerusalem Bible

NKJ   New King James Version (1982)
NLT   New Living Translation
NOR   The Norton NT English Peshitta (1851)
NOY   George Noyes Bible (1869)
NRS   New Revised Standard Version (1989)
PNT   Bishops' New Testament (1595)
QBE   Dead Sea Scrolls Bible Biblical text
ROT   The Rotherham Bible (1999)
RPTE   Revised Patriarchal Greek Orthodox New Testament (2010)
RSV   Revised Standard Version (1952)
RWB   Revised Webster Update (1995) with Codes
TNIV   Today's New International Version
TNK   Jewish Publication Society Tanakh (1985)
TNT   Tyndale New Testament (1534)
WEB   The Webster Bible (1833)
YLT   Young's Literal Translation (1862/1898)

English Translations from Bible Gateway

AMP   Amplified Bible
CEV   Contemporary English Version
EHV   Evangelical Heritage Version
EXB   The Expanded Bible
GNT   Good News Translation
ISV   International Standard Version
JUB   Jubilee Bible
KJ21   King James 21st Century
LEB   the Lexham English Bible
MSG   The Message
NCV   New Century Version
NEB   New English Bible
NIRV   New International Readers Version
NLV   New Life Version
NMB   New Matthew Bible
NTE   NT for Everyone
OJB   Orthodox Jewish Bible
PHL   and J. B. Phillips .
TLB   The Living Bible
TPT   The Passion Translation
VOICE The Voice
WYC   Wycliffe Bible

Biblical Documents

Gen	1, 2Chr	Jer	Nah	Ac	Phlm
Ex	Ezra	Lam	Hab	Rom	Heb
Lev	Neh	Ezek	Zeph	1,2Cor	Jas
Num	Esth	Dan	Hag	Gal	1, 2Pt
Dt	Job	Hos	Zech	Eph	1, 2, 3Jn
Josh	Ps (Pss)	Joel	Mal	Phil	Jude
Judg	Prov	Amos	Mt	Col	Rev
Ruth	Eccl	Obad	Mk	1, 2Th	
1, 2Sam	Song	Jonah	Lk	1, 2Tim	
1, 2Kgs	Isa	Mic	Jn	Titus	

OT Apocrypha

1-4Macc	1Maccabees	Sus	Susanna
Jdt	Judith	Tob	Tobit
Sir	Sirach (Ecclesiasticus)	Wis	Wisdom

Abbreviations for Resources

AB	Anchor Bible Reference Library
ABD	*Anchor Bible Dictionary*. 6 volumes. Doubleday, 1992.
Apoc	Apocrypha
BECNT	Baker Exegetical Commentary on the New Testament
BDAG	Bauer, Danker, Arndt, and Gingrich, *A Greek-English Lexicon of the New Testament and Other Early Christian Literature*. 3rd edition. Chicago, 2000.
BDF	Blass, DeBrunner, Funk, *A Greek Grammar of the New Testament and Other Early Christian Literature*. Chicago, 1961.
BG	Zerwick, Maximilian. *Biblical Greek*. Scripta Pontificii Instituti Biblici. Rome 1963.
BGT	BibleWorks database, a combination of the Nestle-Aland 28th Ed. Greek New Testament (BNT) and Rahlfs' LXX (LXT)
BHS	Elliger, K. and Rudolph, W., (eds.). *Biblia Hebraica Stuttgartensia*. Stuttgart: Deutsche Bibelgesellschaft, 1977.
BW10	BibleWorks version 10. (https://bibleworks.com/)
CCAP	*Conversation Over Coffee with Paul Series*
DJG	*Dictionary of Jesus and the Gospels*. IVP, 1992.
CWP	*Coffee With Paul* (English text Bible study project)
DNTB	*Dictionary of New Testament Background*. IVP, 2000.
DPL	*Dictionary of Paul and His Letters*. IVP, 1993.
IABC	*Institute for the Art of Biblical Conversation*
ISBERev	*International Standard Bible Encyclopedia*. 4 volumes. Eerdmans, 1979-1988.
IVP	Inter-Varsity Press
JBL	*The Journal of Biblical Literature*
JSNT	*The Journal for the Study of the New Testament*

JWSTP	*Jewish Writings of the Second Temple Period: Apocrypha, Pseudepigrapha, Qumran Sectarian Writings, Philo, Josephus.* The Literature of the Jewish People in the Period of the Second Temple and the Talmud. Section 2. CRINT. Fortress, 1984.
Logos	Logos Bible Software (https://www.logos.com/)
LSJ	Liddell, Scott, and Jones. *A Greek English Lexicon.* Oxford, 1968.
LXX	Septuagint (the Greek OT)
Moule	Moule, C. F. D. *An Idiom-Book of the New Testament.* Cambridge, 1963.
NA28	Nestle-Aland. *Novum Testamentum Graece.* 28th edition. Institute for New Testament Textual Research, 2012.
NETS	*A New English Translation of the Septuagint,* by the International Organization of Septuagint and Cognate Studies, Inc., 2007. Online at http://ccat.sas.upenn.edu/nets/edition/
NICTNT	New International Commentary on the NT
NIDB	*The New Interpreters Dictionary of the Bible.* 5 volumes. Abingdon Press, 2009.
NIGTC	New International Greek Testament Commentary
NT	New Testament
NTS	*New Testament Studies*
OT	Old Testament
Pseud	Pseudepigrapha
Rahlfs	Rahlfs, Alfred (ed.). *Septuaginta.* Stuttgart: Deutsche Bibelgesellschaft, 1979.
Robertson	A. T. Robertson, *A Grammar of the Greek New Testament in the Light of Historical Research.* Broadman, 1934.
SBL	Society of Biblical Literature
SPCK	Society for Promoting Christian Knowledge
TDNT	*Theological Dictionary of the New Testament.* 10 volumes. 1964-1976. Ed. by G. Kittel, G. W. Bromiley & G. Friedrich.
TR	Textus Receptus, or "Received Text," the form of the Greek text commonly accepted and in use at the time the KJV was translated in the early 17th century.
UBS4	Aland, Kurt; Black, Matthew; Martini, Carlo M.; Metzger, Bruce M; Wikgren, Allen (Eds.). *The Greek New Testament.* 4th ed. New York: United Bible Societies, 1993.
OT	Old Testament
Wallace	Wallace, Daniel. *Greek Grammar Beyond the Basics.* Zondervan, 1996.

All Other Abbreviations

pl	plural
sg	singular
x	times (as in 7x = 7 times)

Author

GARY D. COLLIER, PhD (Graduate Theological Foundation in association with Oxford University, Christ Church), is director of *The Institute for the Art of Biblical Conversation (IABC)* and the author of a growing list of books, most notably:

- *Graphē in Biblical and Related Literature (2018)*

- *I, Paulos: Shades of Conversation in 1Thessalonians (rev. 2018)*

- *Shades of Biblical Conversation:*
  The Art of Conversing with Biblical Authors (2018)

- *Scripture, Canon, & Inspiration (2012)*

- *The Forgotten Treasure: Reading the Bible Like Jesus (1993)*

For complete author information, go to

BiblicalConversation.COM/gcollier/

.